MENTAL DISABILITY LAW
a primer
Fourth Edition

Authors — **Deborah Zuckerman, Marc Charmatz**
Editors — **John Parry, Deborah Zuckerman**
Production — **Lisa Wunderlich**

The authors want to acknowledge Roy Reynolds, Marc Lampson, and Leonard Tao, who wrote the prior versions of the Primer on which this edition is based.

Published by the Commission on Mental and Physical Disability Law, American Bar Association, 1800 M Street, N.W., Washington, D.C. 20036, (202) 331-2240

This publication was supported by funds from the ABA Fund for Justice and Education.

The material contained herein represents the views of the authors and editors and should not be construed as American Bar Association policy unless adopted pursuant to the Bylaws of the Association.

Copyright © 1992 by the American Bar Association, Washington, D.C.

ISBN 0-89707-798-9

Library of Congress Catalog Number: 92-73324

TABLE OF CONTENTS

PREFACE v

PART I
GETTING STARTED
REPRESENTING PEOPLE WITH MENTAL DISABILITIES

The Importance of Proper Terminology 1
Key Definitions and Terms 2
   Mental Illness (Emotional Disturbance)
   Mental Retardation
   Epilepsy
   Autism
   Learning Disabilities
Why Represent People with Mental Disabilities? 8
   Ethical Considerations for the Attorney 8
   Reasonable Compensation 11
     Statutes 11
       Civil Rights Attorneys' Fees Awards Act
       Rehabilitation Act
       Individuals With Disabilities Education Act
       Americans With Disabilities Act
       Equal Access to Justice Act
       Other Programs
     Significant Cases on Representation 13
Representing a Person With a Mental Disability 16
   Fundamental Concerns 16
   Civil Commitment 17
   Representing Institutionalized People 18

PART II
HIGHLIGHTS OF THE LAW

Involuntary Civil Commitment 20
   Three Approaches to Civil Commitment 21
   Significant Cases 22
   Periodic Review and Release 23
   Outpatient and Preventive Commitment 24
   "Voluntary" and Third Party Commitment 26
Criminal Mental Disability Issues 27
   Civil-Criminal Dichotomy 27
   Trial Competency 28
   Other Criminal Competency Issues 30
      Confessions 30
      Pleas 31
      Sentencing/Death Penalty 31
      Victims/Witnesses 33
   Insanity Defense 33
      Burden & Standard of Proof 35
      Dispositions 36
   Guilty But Mentally Ill 37
   Diminished Capacity 37
   Mentally Disordered Sex Offenders (MDSO) 38
   Expert Assistance 39
Rights Within the Institution 40
   Statutory Rights 41
   Constitutional Rights 41
   Least Restrictive Environment 43
   Treatment Refusals 44
Deinstitutionalization 47
   Constitutional Rights 47
   Post-Youngberg and Pennhurst II 48
   Federal & State Statutes 50
Decisionmaking Rights & Competency 51

 Overview 51
 Guardianship & Conservatorship 52
 Fundamental Decisionmaking Rights 54
  Sexual Rights (Sterilization, Abortion) 55
  Parental Rights 56
  Property & Other Rights 57
  Health Care Decisions 58
   Electroconvulsive Therapy
   Right to Die
 Infants With Severe Disabilities 63
Exclusionary Zoning 64
 State Laws & Policies 64
 Federal Law 66
Employment 67
 Rehabilitation Act 67
 Americans With Disabilities Act 68
 Definitions 69
  Disability 69
  Qualified Individual With A Disability 70
  Reasonable Accommodation 70
 Litigation 71
  Private Right of Action 71
  Section 504 72
  Section 501 74
Education 76
 Individuals With Disabilities Education Act 76
 Section 504 & the ADA 77
 Free, Appropriate, Public Education 77
 Related Services 78
 Placement 79
 Financial Issues 79
 Compensatory Education & Extended School Year 80
 Expulsion of Students 81

Immunity 81
Damages 82
Private Insurance 83
   Coverage 83
   Reimbursement of Service Providers 85
Confidentiality 86
   Duty to Protect 86
   Therapist-Patient Privilege 87
   Impact of Disclosure 89
   Privacy 89
Liability 89
   Residents/Patients 90
   Third Party Liability 91
   Sovereign Immunity & Other Limits 92
Professional Licensing & Discipline 93
Social Security Programs & Medicaid 94
   Social Security 94
      Representative Payee 98
   Medicaid 98

PART III
SPECIAL RESOURCES

ABA Commission on Mental and Physical Disability Law .. 101
   Products & Services 101

Table of Cases 106

PREFACE

Mental disability law has come of age in the past 25 years, particularly with the recent enactment of the Americans With Disabilities Act (ADA). This area of law has grown into a recognized and respected field of practice with universal jurisprudential concerns: individual rights and responsibilities, and limitations on state power. Advocates for people with mental disabilities often speak in terms of securing "rights" for their clients:

- the right to a free, appropriate, public education;
- the right to live and work where one chooses;
- the right to conceive and raise children;
- the right to receive proper, adequate medical care;
- the right to refuse unwanted medical care; and
- the right to be free of physical or drug-induced restraints.

This is only a partial listing. The mental disability field encompasses many facets of the law, substantive and procedural, civil and criminal, constitutional and statutory, state and federal, administrative and judicial. As a lawyer/advocate in this area, you frequently will work in close association with professionals from other disciplines: psychologists, psychiatrists and other medical doctors, educators, social workers, health care workers, administrators, and possibly even architects and urban planners.

One goal of this *Primer* is to make mental disability law more understandable and accessible, not only because we think the legal developments and opportunities are exciting and challenging, but also because we want to increase the availability of competent, effective advocates for people with mental disabilities who tend to be particularly vulnerable and underserved.

To a large degree, clients with mental disabilities (mental illnesses and developmental disabilities) are likely to be poor, undereducated and in poor health; to have inadequate housing and other community supports; and to have a limited ability to effectively communicate their needs and desires. The clients' mental condition does not necessarily *cause* these circumstances, but the clients often have been the victims of discrimination in employment or in public entitlement programs, inadequate and inappropriate educational opportunities, inadequate and uninformed medical care, and/or society's prejudices and misconceptions. Legal remedies often become the only available means for redressing these grievances.

This *Primer* is designed to point new lawyers, those with experience in other fields, and other advocates in the right direction so they may provide competent representation and other assistance to clients with mental disabilities. The *Primer* also is a good starting point for graduate students whose courses of study in law, medicine, psychology, nursing, social work, and related disciplines encompass mental disability law. Given the broad range of topics involved in this area of law, however, the *Primer* cannot be the definitive source, or even a comprehensive practice manual, in each of the areas discussed. Rather, this publication seeks to alert the reader to the primary areas of concern; the major issues within each of those areas; the principal constitutional, statutory, and case law developments in each area; and additional sources of assistance.

We strongly encourage legal practitioners to consult the highlighted cases and other resources to achieve a broader understanding of particular issues. Please note, that each court decision discussed in the *Primer* is given with its published or unpublished cite, as well as a volume and page number on which the case was analyzed in the *Mental Disability Law Reporter* (1976-1983) or the *Mental and Physical Disability Law Reporter* (1984-present), e.g., 5 MDLR 21, 16 MPDLR 300, published by the American Bar Association's Commission on Mental and Physical Disability Law. A compilation of case summaries, as well as the text of all the cases, articles, statutes, and regulations cited in this *Primer* is available from the Commission.

Part I of the *Primer* addresses preliminary considerations regarding the scope of mental disability law, defines key terms, explains why an advocate would want to represent the interests of people with mental disabilities, and discusses how to provide such representation. Part II reviews major federal legislative initiatives and constitutional mandates, and highlights specific subjects such as civil commitment; criminal law issues, e.g., trial competency, insanity defense; employment discrimination; the right to an education; health care, including the rights to receive and to refuse medication and other treatment; and professional liability. Part III presents information on the Commission's publications and services.

PART I
Getting Started
Representing People With Mental Disabilities

The Importance of Proper Terminology

All practitioners entering the mental disability field face unfamiliar territory. Terminology is the initial obstacle that attorneys/advocates will encounter in trying to achieve a full understanding of the field.

Language plays a critical role in mental disability law. The definitions of many terms and phrases used in the field may be imprecise or disputed. One statute defines a term one way and a related statute may define the same term somewhat differently. Health care professionals and advocates may not agree among themselves on even the most fundamental concepts such as mental illness, mental retardation, disability, and handicap. In addition, many terms like insanity and competency have different connotations in the legal and medical fields.

Beyond merely avoiding confusion, however, the choice of words is critical because a client's fate may rest on terminology, i.e., the labels that medical and legal institutions and practitioners attach to the client. These labels may determine clients' rights, the benefits to which they may be entitled, the facilities and institutions that are open or closed to them, the kind of care and treatment they will receive, and whether their liberty and choices can be restricted without their consent.

Lawyers/advocates beginning to practice in this area should also be sensitive to the language they use in counseling and representing clients. Cultural biases are embedded in our language and our choice of words may betray misunderstandings, preconceptions, and prejudices. We thus must examine our language carefully to avoid perpetuating harmful stereotypes and misassumptions. Moreover, a lack of awareness, or insensitivity to the negative connotations of certain words and phrases, may be interpreted as disrespect for one's clients, their family, and their friends.

Although reasonable people may and do disagree on the best way to refer to people with disabilities, the most accepted approach is to use "people first" language. In this formulation, a person is not characterized by the fact that he or she has a disability, but is viewed as a person first, who possesses many different characteristics, one of which is a disability. Thus, we do not refer to someone as mentally ill, mentally retarded, or as an epileptic, but rather, as a person with a mental illness, with mental retardation, or with epilepsy.

Key Definitions and Terms

This *Primer* uses the term *mental disability* as a convenient shorthand for a group of impairments that have mental or cognitive elements and are treated similarly within the framework of our laws. Mental disability can be divided into two branches, one dealing with mental illness, and the other with developmental disabilities. These two subgroups overlap and thus are not entirely separable.

Mental illness is a group of illnesses, including both mental and cognitive disorders, while *developmental disabilities* are a variety of conditions grouped by their severity and age of onset. The latter category includes physical, cognitive, and mental illnesses that begin by early adulthood, are likely to continue indefinitely, and produce a severe functional impairment, in that they adversely affect one or more of the individual's major life activities.

Federal legislation originally defined developmental disability to include only mental retardation, epilepsy, autism, and cerebral palsy. Subsequently, a broader, more functionally oriented definition was adopted, emphasizing the impairment's severity, its onset before the age of 22, and its likelihood of continuing throughout the person's lifetime.

The following definitions were originally excerpted from *The Legal Rights of Handicapped Persons,* Robert L. Burgdorf, Jr., ed. (1980). In some instances, new information has been used to update these definitions. These terms were chosen because they provide an overview of the complex technical language used in mental disability law. This list is a good starting point, but is neither exhaustive nor without limitations. Another important source of information is the *Diagnostic and Statistical Manual of Mental*

Disorders published by the American Psychiatric Association. The revised third edition, DSM-III-R, acknowledged that:

> Although this manual provides a classification of mental disorders, there is no satisfactory definition that specifies precise boundaries for the concept "mental disorder" (also true for such concepts as physical disorder and mental and physical health). Nevertheless, it is useful to present concepts that have influenced the decision to include certain conditions in DSM-III as mental disorders and to exclude others.

(1) Mental Illness (Emotional Disturbance)

Disorders of mental processes, which may be evidenced by disordered thinking, perceptual difficulties, delusions, hallucinations, mood disturbances, and impairments in social and vocational functioning and self-care. Severe mental illnesses include schizophrenia, bipolar disorder, and severe depression.

Causes

Many are unknown. For some conditions, prevalent beliefs include theories of genetic predisposition, shifts in brain biochemistry, slow-acting viral infection, brain trauma, or response to traumatic events. In addition, some familial patterns have been established. Schizophrenia and bipolar disorder generally have an early adult onset, while severe depression can occur at anytime throughout a person's lifetime.

Treatment

  (a) <u>Standard measures</u>

    (1) Administration of medication

    (2) Psychotherapy

    (3) Various behavior modification techniques

    (4) Rehabilitation interventions, such as assistance with housing, employment, and education

    (5) Self-help and peer support groups

(b) <u>Less common measures</u>

   (1) Psychosurgery

   (2) Hypnosis

   (3) Electroconvulsive therapy (ECT)

Miscellaneous

No meaningful distinction can be made between the terms *mental illness* and *emotional disturbance*, although there is a tendency to use the latter term with respect to children in the education context. *Insanity*, a legal term generally used in the criminal context, refers to a mental condition that excuses a person from criminal liability, usually because it makes him or her unable to appreciate the wrongfulness of an act, and/or to control his or her behavior.

Additional Information

    National Mental Health Association
    1021 Prince Street
    Alexandria, VA 22314-2971
    (703) 684-7722

    American Psychiatric Association
    1401 K Street, N.W.
    Washington, D.C. 20005
    (202) 682-6000

    American Psychological Association
    750 First Street, N.E.
    Washington, D.C. 20002-4242
    (202) 336-5500

(2) Mental Retardation

"Mental retardation refers to substantial limitations in present functioning. It is characterized by significantly subaverage intellectual functioning, existing concurrently with related limitations in two or more of the following applicable adaptive skill areas: communication, self-care, home living, social skills, community use, self-direction, health and safety, functional academics, leisure, and work. Mental retardation manifests before age 18." American Association on Mental Retardation (AAMR),

Mental Retardation: Definition, Classification, and System of Supports, 9th ed. 1992. AAMR indicates that a diagnosis of mental retardation requires an IQ below 70-75, an onset age of 18 or below, and significant disabilities in two or more adaptive skill areas.

Causes

Although many causes of mental retardation remain unknown, some of the known causes include:

(a) Biological

   (1) Down syndrome - results from an extra chromosome (47 instead of 46); causes identifiable physical characteristics and usually causes delayed physical and intellectual development

   (2) Phenylketonuria (PKU) - results in the body's inability to properly metabolize the amino acid phenylalanine; a build up of the amino acid in the blood causes brain damage and mental retardation

   (3) Tay-Sachs - a metabolic error in processing fats that leads to severe mental retardation and death

   (4) Tuberous sclerosis - a progressive neurological disorder characterized by seizures, mental retardation, tumors, and lesions

(b) Injuries

   (1) Brain and head injuries from accidents, falls, near-drownings, child abuse

   (2) Accidents or other physical injury to the fetus, as well as injury during the birth process, especially oxygen deprivation

(c) Infections/toxins

   (1) Viruses such as rubella, meningitis, measles, contracted by the mother during pregnancy or by the individual him or herself after birth

   (2) Use of alcohol, cigarettes, other drugs during pregnancy, e.g., fetal alcohol syndrome (FAS)

(3) Sexually transmitted diseases, such as AIDS

(4) Lead poisoning

(d) Socioeconomic & environmental factors

(1) Some studies show that poverty is a determinant in 75-80% of people with mild mental retardation with no organic cause

(2) Poor nutrition, sanitation, pre- and/or postnatal care; impure water, unsafe housing (e.g., lead-based paint)

Treatment

PKU can be controlled by diet. Otherwise, educational, vocational, and other support services are available to maximize the potential of persons with mental retardation and to facilitate their integration into society as much as possible.

Additional Information

American Association on Mental Retardation
1719 Kalorama Road, N.W.
Washington, D.C. 20009
(202) 387-1968

The Arc (A National Organization on Mental Retardation)
500 East Border Street
Arlington, TX 76010
(817) 261-6003

(3) Epilepsy

A chronic brain disorder characterized by recurrent seizures. A seizure is an abnormal electrical discharge by nerve cells in the brain which typically results in an interruption of consciousness and also may cause involuntary convulsive muscle movements. Seizures caused by something external to the brain itself, e.g., hypoglycemia (low blood sugar), do not constitute epilepsy.

Causes

Brain injuries before, during or after birth; brain tumors and abscesses; nutritional deficiencies; fever; certain diseases and congenital disorders. The cause often is unknown.

Treatment

Anticonvulsant drugs, surgery

Additional Information

> Epilepsy Foundation of America
> 4351 Garden City Drive
> Suite 406
> Landover, MD 20785
> (301) 459-3700

(4) Autism

"Autism is a severely incapacitating lifelong developmental disability that typically appears during the first three years of life." Some behavioral symptoms include: disturbances in the rate of appearance of physical, social, and language skills; abnormal responses to sensations (any one or a combination of senses or responses are affected, i.e., vision, hearing, touch, balance, taste, smell, reaction to pain, the way a child holds his or her body); speech and language are absent or delayed, while specific thinking capabilities may be present; abnormal ways of relating to people, objects, events. The severe form of the syndrome may include extreme self-injurious, repetitive, highly unusual, and aggressive behavior. This information was provided by the Autism Society of America, which cautions on the importance of distinguishing "autism from retardation or mental disorders since diagnostic confusion may result in referral to inappropriate and ineffective treatment techniques."

Causes

A neurological disorder that affects brain functioning. It may occur by itself or with other disorders that affect brain functioning, such as viral infections, metabolic disturbances, and epilepsy.

Treatment

Early diagnosis and intervention are vital to the child's development. Special education programs using behavioral methods have proved to be the most helpful.

Additional Information
>Autism Society of America
>8601 Georgia Avenue
>Suite 503
>Silver Spring, MD 20910
>(301) 565-0433

(5) Learning Disabilities

A disorder in one or more of the basic psychological processes involved in understanding or using spoken or written language, manifested by a significant discrepancy between intellectual ability and actual achievement in listening, thinking, speaking, reading, writing, spelling, or performing arithmetic computations. Examples include dyslexia, hyperactivity, hypoactivity, and developmental aphasia. Learning problems primarily attributable to visual, hearing, or motor impairments, mental retardation or emotional disturbance, or environmental, cultural, or economic disadvantages are not considered learning disabilities.

Causes
Organic brain dysfunction and unknown reasons

Treatment
Educational programs, special diets, and medication

Additional Information
>Learning Disabilities Association of America
>4156 Library Road
>Pittsburgh, PA 15234
>(412) 341-1515

Why Represent People With Mental Disabilities?

Ethical Considerations for the Attorney

Few attorneys would question representation for a corporate client, an injured automobile driver, a property owner seeking an easement, or a criminal defendant. These and similar clients are the core of many law practices and they generally have access to representation. This is not true for persons with mental disabilities who, historically, have needed and not received zealous legal advocacy. Even with protection and advocacy programs for persons with mental illnesses or developmental disabilities, a significant unmet need remains.

People with mental disabilities often are relegated to the margins of society: ignored, forgotten, or feared. The legal advocate soon will discover that societal attitudes toward this client group often interfere with the recognition of these clients' legal and human rights.

Ethical considerations in representing clients with mental disabilities increase in complexity in relation to the severity of the client's disability. Ordinarily, the command of the ABA Model Rules of Professional Conduct that the attorney "should act with commitment and dedication to the interests of the client and with zeal in advocacy upon the client's behalf" is straightforward. (Rule 1.3) Many clients with mild or moderate disabilities are fully capable of understanding legal proceedings and expressing their wishes and interests regarding those proceedings.

The attorney faces a much more difficult situation when the client has a severe or profound disability or is heavily medicated. These clients may be unable to express their desires, voice their complaints, or argue for their interests. Zealous advocacy may conflict with the interests of the clients' relatives, guardians, or the state. Such advocacy might even conflict with the attorney's interests, where representation is time-consuming, confusing, or financially risky.

Some of the ethical considerations, legal and nonlegal, regarding the responsibility to represent clients with mental disabilities are based on constitutional mandates, federal statutes, state practices, and private bar initiatives.

A constitutional right to legal representation has been established in criminal proceedings and, in many jurisdictions, in civil commitment and guardianship proceedings as well. In 1988, the American Bar Association's House of Delegates adopted a resolution stating that "[c]ounsel as advocate for the [guardianship] respondent should be appointed in every case, to be supplanted by respondent's private counsel if the respondent prefers." In addition, in *Vitek v. Jones*, 445 U.S. 480 (1980), 4 MDLR 152, the U.S. Supreme Court held that prisoners being transferred to mental hospitals must be represented by qualified, independent advocates, not necessarily lawyers. Similarly, juveniles whose parents are seeking their "voluntary" commitment to institutions are entitled, at a minimum, to independent reviewers, who may be the admitting physicians. *Parham v. J.R.*, 442 U.S. 584 (1979), 3 MDLR 231.

Beyond these cases, however, there are no commonly accepted constitutional mandates regarding the right of people with mental disabilities to an attorney's services in civil actions, except perhaps, adults with mental disabilities who face the termination of their parental rights. See *Lassiter v. Dep't of Social Servs. of Durham County*, 452 U.S. 18 (1981), 5 MDLR 235. Most laws conferring a civil right to counsel are found at the state level, and usually cover only extremely important issues such as civil commitment and guardianship. Even where a right to representation in civil matters exists, however, its implementation tends to be quite a haphazard affair, depending on both the actual statutory mandate and the means to assure that authorized representation is provided.

The first amendment provides additional evidence of a right to counsel. For example, the First Circuit examined a legal advocacy program's first amendment rights to communicate with and represent clients with mental disabilities. The court noted that "it is now clear . . . [these organizations] . . . have first amendment rights which in appropriate circumstances, may permit them to seek out clients and initiate litigation." *Developmental Disabilities Advocacy Center, Inc. v. Melton*, 689 F.2d 281 (lst Cir. 1982), 7 MDLR 13. More recent decisions have affirmed that attorneys working for the federally-funded Protection and Advocacy (P&A) organizations are entitled to access to patients, and that an institution's actions in restricting access interfered with residents' rights to an effective P&A system. See, e.g., *Mississippi Protection & Advocacy Sys. v. Cotten*, 929 F.2d 1054 (5th Cir. 1991), 15 MPDLR 368; *Robbins v. Budke*, 739 F. Supp. 1479 (D.N.M. 1990), 14 MPDLR 358 (overly burdensome restrictions on patient access to P&A advocates and advocates' access to patients' records violate first and fourteenth amendments); and *Wisconsin Coalition for Advocacy, Inc. v. Gudeman*, No. 90CV05918 (Wis. Cir. Ct. May 2, 1990), 14 MPDLR 358.

While the legal profession recognizes a general obligation to make legal counsel available to everyone, the final responsibility for providing legal counsel to those who are unable to pay rests with individual attorneys. Under the Model Rules of Professional Conduct, Rule 6.1, lawyers are expected to deliver pro bono services, but no disciplinary measures are taken against those attorneys who fail to do so.

Reasonable Compensation

There are several ways in which attorneys can generate income by representing people with mental disabilities in both civil and criminal matters. In addition to the pro bono and legal services programs that provide essential legal representation, several statutes and government programs authorize attorneys' fees. The federal civil rights statutes discussed below already have led to many substantial fee awards — some for hundreds of thousands of dollars at hourly rates of $100 or more.

Statutes

Five separate, but very similar, federal provisions permit the award of attorneys' fees in suits that involve clients with disabilities. Each of these provisions is limited by the requirement that one must be the "prevailing party" in order to receive an award. Who has prevailed in litigation is not always evident, however.

Civil Rights Attorneys' Fees Awards Act

The Civil Rights Attorneys' Fees Awards Act, 42 U.S.C. §1988, helps to enforce the Civil Rights Act of 1964 by giving citizens the opportunity to recover the costs of vindicating their civil rights. Historically, this section has provided the broadest opportunity for awards.

Rehabilitation Act

Section 505 of the Rehabilitation Act, 29 U.S.C. §794a, was designed to ensure that a prevailing party in an action to enforce discrimination complaints in programs or activities receiving federal financial assistance can recover reasonable attorneys' fees as part of the litigation costs. Thus, §505 primarily provides fee awards to plaintiffs who have prevailed on their Rehabilitation Act claims.

Individuals with Disabilities Education Act

Congress amended the Individuals with Disabilities Education Act (IDEA) to provide a discretionary award of attorneys' fees. The Handicapped Children's Protection Act (HCPA), 20 U.S.C. §1415(e), provides fee awards to plaintiffs who have prevailed on their claims that a school district or a state educational agency did not provide a free, appropriate public education. The HCPA also provides that a fee cannot be awarded for legal services performed after a written settlement offer has been made. Thus, parents would not be entitled to attorneys' fees if the administrative or judicial relief they obtained was no more favorable than the settlement offer. *See* 20 U.S.C. §1415(e)(4)(D). This concession to school districts and state educational agencies is not found in any of the other attorneys' fee statutes discussed herein.

Americans with Disabilities Act

The Americans with Disabilities Act (ADA), 42 U.S.C. §12101 et seq., provides for attorneys' fees to prevailing parties in three separate provisions: (a) under Title I, 42 U.S.C. §12117, dealing with employment, as set forth in the Civil Rights Act; (b) under Title II, 42 U.S.C. §12133, dealing with state and local government services, as set forth in §505 of the Rehabilitation Act, 29 U.S.C. §794a; and (c) under Title III, 42 U.S.C. §12188, dealing with public accommodations.

Equal Access to Justice Act

The Equal Access to Justice Act (EAJA), 28 U.S.C. §2412, was established to correct the inequity that existed because private citizens were rarely allowed to collect costs against the federal government. The doctrine of sovereign immunity protected the U.S. government from being sued for damages of any kind, without legislative permission. The EAJA allows prevailing parties to recover reasonable costs "unless the court finds that the position of the United States was substantially justified or that special circumstances make an award unjust." 28 U.S.C. §2412(d)(1)(A).

Other Programs

The Developmental Disabilities Assistance and Bill of Rights Act,

42 U.S.C. §6000 et seq., established advocacy services for clients with developmental disabilities. The Protection and Advocacy for Mentally Ill Individuals Act, 42 U.S.C. §10801 et seq., provided federal funding for states to establish programs to investigate abuse or neglect of people with mental illnesses and to pursue legal and administrative remedies on their behalf. Legal assistance is also available through the Legal Services Corporation.

Finally, several categories of cases can generate sufficient awards to support fees for litigation: representing individuals in Social Security disability benefit disputes; handling professional liability and malpractice claims; and pursuing workers' compensation and other work-related disability benefit matters.

Significant Cases on Representation

The U.S. Supreme Court has decided several cases involving the attorneys' fee provisions discussed above. In *Hensley v. Eckerhart,* 461 U.S. 424 (1983), 7 MDLR 307, the High Court declared that under 42 U.S.C. §1988, attorneys' fees should be reduced whenever the plaintiffs are not completely successful in achieving their intended result. The overall "results obtained" are the most important factor in awarding fees. Thus, plaintiffs who achieve substantial success should not have their fees reduced merely because they did not prevail on each of their claims.

In *Blum v. Stenson,* 465 U.S. 886 (1984), 8 MPDLR 317, the Court held that under §1988, "reasonable fees" must be calculated according to prevailing market rates in the particular community in which the litigation occurs. The Court stated that "Congress did not intend the calculation of fee awards to vary depending on whether plaintiff was represented by private counsel or by a nonprofit legal services corporation." This holding made it possible for nonprofit legal aid organizations to receive fee awards equal to the fees charged by private law firms. The Court limited any additional "upward adjustment" of attorneys' fee awards, however, by requiring that evidence in the record demonstrate the complexity of the litigation, the novelty of the issues, the high quality of the representation, or the "great benefit" to the plaintiffs' class.

Several other U.S. Supreme Court cases have placed modest limits on fee awards. In *Evans v. Jeff D.,* 475 U.S. 717 (1986), 10

MPDLR 207, the Court held that §1988 allowed a federal court to approve a settlement in which attorneys' fees were waived in exchange for broad injunctive relief. Three dissenting justices felt that this precedent would deter attorneys from representing plaintiffs in civil rights actions.

In *North Carolina Dep't of Transp. v. Crest St. Community Council, Inc.*, 479 U.S. 6 (1986), 10 MPDLR 572, the High Court held that fees could not be awarded under §1988 for the negotiated settlement of an administrative complaint. And, recently, in *West Virginia Univ. Hosps. v. Casey*, 111 S. Ct. 1138 (1991), 15 MPDLR 296, the U.S. Supreme Court held that a court's authority to award reasonable attorneys' fees under §1988 does not include expert witness fees. Attorneys' fees and expert fees are distinct expense items and, in other laws, where Congress has wanted to shift both types of expense to the losing party, it has done so explicitly.

The U.S. Supreme Court also restricted the award of attorneys' fees under §1988 and §505 of the Rehabilitation Act if plaintiffs had an alternative remedy under the IDEA (formerly the Education for All Handicapped Children Act). *Smith v. Robinson*, 468 U.S. 992 (1984), 8 MPDLR 392. Congress overturned *Smith*, however, enacting the Handicapped Children's Protection Act of 1986. 20 U.S.C. §1415(e). The amendment to the IDEA allows attorneys' fees for parents who prevailed in judicial proceedings brought under the IDEA.

A number of lower courts have held that parents who prevail at an administrative due process hearing can apply for attorneys' fees even though a court did not consider the merits of the case. *Eggers v. Bullitt*, 854 F.2d 892 (6th Cir. 1988), 13 MPDLR 63; *Duane M. v. Orleans Parish School Bd.*, 861 F.2d 115 (5th Cir. 1988), 13 MPDLR 63; and *Moore v. District of Columbia*, 866 F.2d 335 (D.C. Cir. 1989), 14 MPDLR 68. Courts have also held that parents are prevailing parties entitled to attorneys' fees even though they settled a lawsuit prior to a due process hearing. *Barlow-Gresham Union High School Dist. No. 2 v. Mitchell*, 940 F.2d 1280 (9th Cir. 1991), 15 MPDLR 608. *But see Johnson v. Bismarck Public School Dist.*, 949 F.2d 1000 (8th Cir. 1991), 16 MPDLR 217 (parents who settled administrative complaint prior to due process hearing not entitled to attorneys' fees because parents unreasonably protracted the dispute).

The U.S. Supreme Court also has decided cases dealing with attorneys' fees in Social Security matters. In *Bowen v. Galbreath*, 485 U.S. 74 (1988), 12 MPDLR 187, the Court ruled 8-0 that a federal district court did not have the authority to order the Secretary of Health and Human Services to offset past-due Supplemental Security Income (SSI) benefits to pay the attorneys' fees of a successful claimant's attorney. It was more important to protect the client's benefits than to ensure that lawyers received their fees in a timely manner.

In *Sullivan v. Hudson*, 490 U.S. 877 (1989), 13 MPDLR 400, the U.S. Supreme Court upheld an award of attorneys' fees under the EAJA for the representation of a disability claimant in a Social Security administrative proceeding. When a federal district court retains jurisdiction of a civil action and contemplates entering a final judgment following the completion of administrative proceedings, a claimant may collect EAJA fees for work done at the administrative level.

The U.S. Supreme court recently ruled that for purposes of the EAJA, a "final judgment" upon which attorneys' fees may be awarded is a judgment that is rendered by a court, not an administrative body. Thus, the 30-day period within which a prevailing party must request attorneys' fees begins to run after a court renders a non-appealable final judgment. The Court also held that only two kinds of remands can be made in Social Security disability cases (referred to as "sentence four" or "sentence six" remands), and that the type of remand determines whether a judgment is final for purposes of seeking attorneys' fees. *Melkonyan v. Sullivan*, 111 S. Ct. 2157 (1991), 15 MPDLR 407.

In order to be awarded attorneys' fees under the EAJA, a prevailing party must show that the Secretary of Health & Human Services was not substantially justified in denying benefits. For example, in *Williams v. Bowen*, 934 F.2d 221 (9th Cir. 1991), 15 MPDLR 516, the Ninth Circuit held that the Secretary's position was substantially justified because the claimant's psychiatric evidence was ambiguous and the medical testimony concerning her disabilities was not dispositive.

Other frequently litigated EAJA issues include adjustment to the statutory limit of $75 per hour to account for inflation or other extenuating circumstances, *see, e.g., May v. Sullivan,* 936 F.2d 176 (4th Cir. 1991), 15 MPDLR 516; *Trinidad v. Secretary of Health & Human Servs.,* 935 F.2d 13 (1st Cir. 1991), 15 MPDLR 516; *Sullivan v. Sullivan,* 958 F.2d 574 (4th Cir. 1992), 16 MPDLR 330; and whether, in light of *Melkonyan,* a remand is a sentence four or sentence six remand and thus, whether a fee petition is timely. *See, e.g., Gutierrez v. Sullivan,* 953 F.2d 579 (10th Cir. 1992), 16 MPDLR 327; *Hudson v. Sullivan,* 779 F. Supp. 37 (W.D. Pa. 1991), 16 MPDLR 328; and *Dow v. Sullivan,* 774 F. Supp. 46 (D. Me. 1991), 16 MPDLR 83.

Representing a Person With a Mental Disability

Many issues arise when discussing how to represent a client with a mental disability — who is the client, what precise disability is involved, and what ethical or legal considerations apply. The client's partial or more complete incapacity introduces other complex problems.

Fundamental Concerns

The attorney often faces two fundamental concerns in representing clients with a mental disability. They involve the attorney's posture with regard to the attorney-client relationship, and the skills needed to communicate effectively with a client who has special needs in order to determine the client's point of view and desired action. Attorneys generally have played two types of roles in representing allegedly incapacitated clients. In the traditional role, the attorney protected the client's "best interests," while in the more modern approach, the attorney zealously advocated the client's expressed or implied wishes, regardless of what the attorney perceived as the client's best interests.

Consistent with the ABA's Model Rules of Professional Conduct, the legal profession has largely resolved the best interests vs. zealous advocacy debate in favor of zealous advocacy (*see* Rule 1.3 above). In addition, the Model Rules state that if a "client's ability to make adequately considered decisions in connection with the representation is impaired . . . because of . . . mental disability . . .

the lawyer shall, as far as reasonably possible, maintain a normal client-lawyer relationship with the client." (Rule 1.14) The Comment to the rule states that the lawyer-client relationship is based on the assumption that clients, when properly advised and assisted, are capable of making decisions about important matters. "When the client . . . suffers from a mental disorder or disability, however, maintaining the ordinary client-lawyer relationship may not be possible in all respects. . . . Nevertheless, a client lacking legal competence often has the ability to understand, deliberate upon, and reach conclusions about matters affecting the client's own well-being." This Rule advises that attorneys "may seek the appointment of a guardian or take other protective action with respect to a client only when the lawyer reasonably believes the client cannot adequately act in the client's own interest."

It also is important to realize that the advocate's position vis-a-vis his or her client may depend on the circumstances of the case. In the civil commitment context, the advocate may be called upon to argue vigorously that the client does not meet the criteria that would subject him or her to state-imposed liberty restrictions. In the context of entitlements, however, the advocate will argue that the client is in fact among those for whom such entitlements were intended. In the latter situation the attorney's role is much clearer, since the objective is to obtain more benefits for the client.

Civil Commitment

A dispute continues within the legal profession concerning whether to proceed according to the client's wishes, or the attorney's view of what is best for the client. This is particularly true in civil commitment cases. The practitioner's role may be affected by whether the state seeks to commit the client under the state's *parens patriae* power or its police power. Whether commitment is viewed as a process of securing treatment — the "medical model" — or as a process of depriving a person of his or her liberty — the "legal model" — also may affect the posture the practitioner assumes.

In general, courts that have addressed the issue have recognized a constitutional right to counsel in civil commitment proceedings, based on the Supreme Court's decisions in *Minnesota ex rel.*

Pearson v. Probate Court, 309 U.S. 270, 276 (1940), and *In re Gault*, 387 U.S. 1 (1967). The author of "Right to Counsel in Civil Commitment Proceedings," 9 MPDLR 230, argues that the significant differences that exist between criminal trials and civil commitment proceedings warrant the use of different standards for determining whether effective assistance of counsel has been provided in the two different types of cases. The author offers specific suggestions about what constitutes effective counsel in civil commitment proceedings.

In "The Role of Counsel in the Civil Commitment Process: A Theoretical Framework," 84 *Yale L.J.* 1540 (1975), the author forcefully argues that counsel should play an adversarial role, even in situations where others have argued there is a danger that successful advocacy will deprive the client of needed assistance. The article suggests that this due process concern is counterbalanced by the fact that the process often is skewed in favor of commitment.

To encourage and support improved legal representation for persons involved in civil commitment proceedings, the ABA's Commission on Mental and Physical Disability Law developed training materials to educate lawyers and judges about the civil commitment process. The training manual contains three sections: the largest section, targeted to the respondent's counsel, promotes an advocacy role for the attorney; the other two sections address specific concerns of the state's attorney and the judge. An accompanying videotape introduces the civil commitment process and illustrates both the serious restrictions on liberty that follow involuntary commitment, and the elements that comprise proper legal representation and the commitment hearing itself. *See* p. 104 for additional information on these materials.

Representing Institutionalized People

The advocate faces similar problems in representing a person with a mental disability who has been institutionalized. "Legal Advocacy for Persons in Mental Hospitals," 5 MDLR 274, discusses the division of opinion between "best interests" representation and adversarial advocacy. The article is a "point-counterpoint" between three members of the bar involved in mental disability law who discuss four basic areas of conflict: How should the demand for legal services in an institutional setting be measured? How can that demand best be met given limited resources? What criteria should be used to measure the quality of legal representation? What is the proper role of the attorney in this particular environment? In "Representing Institutionalized Mentally Retarded Persons," 7 MDLR 49, the authors discuss practical considerations in representing institutionalized clients with mental disabilities. Of particular interest is their discussion of the typical difficulties involved in interviewing institutionalized clients, and some practical ways of overcoming those difficulties.

The most significant barrier to effective representation of institutionalized persons with mental disabilities may be the lawyer's reaction. Some lawyers may see no point in seeking direction from a client with a mental disability when in fact, almost all clients have something to contribute to the lawyer's understanding of the case. Ascertaining the preferences and current situation of a person with a mental disability may not be an easy task. Overcoming these communication difficulties through technological advances such as language boards may assist clients who are unable to speak. Ultimately, however, the attorneys must adapt their own style of communicating to their client's ability to understand. This practical approach is reinforced by the "Client Interview Form," found at 7 MDLR 52, and a guide to help lawyers and advocates in their efforts to represent institutionalized persons with mental retardation, 7 MDLR 53.

Finally, in "Representing the Medicated Client," 7 MDLR 55, a practicing attorney addresses one of the most difficult areas in mental disability law — the general effects of medication on behavior, and the lawyer's need to perform an in-depth investigation of the effects of a particular client's medications in order to make informed decisions concerning representation. For example, these medications may cause a "client's sudden change in instructions, listless demeanor on the witness stand or convulsive, nervous mannerisms during an interview."

Part II
Highlights of the Law

Involuntary Civil Commitment

Involuntary civil commitment is the process by which individuals with mental illnesses or other mental impairments, e.g., developmental disabilities, substance abuse, are forced to receive care and treatment, usually in an inpatient setting. The legal standards for involuntary commitment vary from state to state, but the laws typically require a mental disorder that results in people being dangerous to themselves or others, or less commonly, gravely disabled or unable to meet their basic needs.

The process usually is initiated when a third party (petitioner) files a petition asking a court to commit the individual (respondent). To issue an extended involuntary commitment order, the court must hold a hearing and find that the individual meets the jurisdiction's commitment standard. An emergency evaluation or a 72-hour commitment may be ordered without a hearing.

The civil commitment process received close scrutiny during the 1960s, 70s and early 80s, resulting in increased constitutional and statutory protections for proposed patients. More recently, however, there has been a movement to dilute some of the legal standards in order to allow compulsory treatment of persons with mental illness, developmental disabilities, or substance abuse, who are not dangerous to themselves or others. These competing trends have been accompanied by a growing awareness of the importance of due process in commitment hearings, particularly access to competent counsel.

While there is uniformity among the states concerning representation by counsel in commitment hearings, there is diversity in practically all other aspects of the commitment process. This diversity is found in the three leading approaches to involuntary civil commitment that emerged during the 1970s and 80s. A fourth view, espoused most notably by Thomas Szasz, holds that if the mental health system is ever to have credibility, all involuntary services must be abolished.

Three Approaches to Civil Commitment

In 1977, the Mental Health Law Project published "Legal Issues in Mental Health Care: Proposals for Change," 2 MDLR 267, proposing a rigorous due process model of rights protection for persons facing involuntary treatment or commitment, which would require "evidence of overt dangerousness to others before an extended commitment could be ordered."

In 1982, the American Psychiatric Association responded with a model law emphasizing the need for treatment to achieve personal autonomy. Only some of the Mental Health Law Project's due process protections were included, and much broader substantive commitment standards were proposed. Also, there was no post-commitment right to refuse treatment, because the respondent was presumed to be incapable of making sound treatment decisions. Stromberg & Stone, "A Model State Law on Civil Commitment of the Mentally Ill," 20 *Harv. J. on Legis.* 275 (1983).

In 1986, the National Center for State Courts issued "Guidelines for Involuntary Civil Commitment," 10 MPDLR 409, which were intended to better implement existing state laws. The guidelines balanced the rights of persons with mental disabilities against other important societal concerns and, to some extent, were both a counterpoint to, and a successful integration of, the model statutes discussed above.

The 50 guidelines included recommendations for: better coordination between legal agencies and mental health providers; improved law enforcement training; precommitment screening; effective legal representation; improved court hearings; the use of dispositional alternatives; court orders that specify the treatment that is to be provided and the place where it will be provided; and legal representation for the client after the commitment proceedings conclude.

Significant Cases

The first landmark civil commitment case during the 1970s was *Lessard v. Schmidt,* 349 F. Supp. 1078 (E.D. Wis. 1972), *vacated and remanded on other grounds,* 414 U.S. 473 (1974), *redecided,* 379 F. Supp. 1376 (E.D. Wis. 1974), *vacated and remanded on other grounds,* 421 U.S. 957 (1975), *redecided,* 413 F. Supp. 1318 (E.D. Wis. 1976), 1 MDLR 32. It established two basic principles: the state must provide less restrictive alternatives to long-term institutionalization, where such alternatives exist; and there can be no involuntary commitment without a finding of "dangerousness" to self or others. Both concepts have gained significant footholds in the law, although neither commands universal acceptance.

Several years later, in *Addington v. Texas,* 441 U.S. 418 (1979), 3 MDLR 164, the U.S. Supreme Court held that the fourteenth amendment requires "clear and convincing evidence" that commitment criteria have been met, before someone can be involuntarily hospitalized. While rejecting the notion that involuntary civil commitment should be equated with criminal incarceration, the Court recognized that such proceedings have far more serious implications than ordinary civil proceedings.

The U.S. Supreme Court held, in *O'Connor v. Donaldson,* 422 U.S. 563 (1975), 1 MDLR 336, that warehousing people in institutions is unconstitutional. Custodial confinement, without something more, is not justified for nondangerous individuals who are capable of living in freedom by themselves or with the help of family and friends. While failing to endorse a constitutional right to treatment or habilitation, this case laid the basis for federal and state courts to recognize various forms of the least restrictive alternative concept.

O'Connor v. Donaldson also helped to focus attention on the dangerousness standard, which a majority of jurisdictions now require. In fact, a recent Supreme Court decision cited *O'Connor v. Donaldson* and indicated that dangerousness may be a constitutional requirement. *Zinermon v. Burch,* 494 U.S. 113 (1990), 14 MPDLR 116. "The involuntary placement process serves to guard against the confinement of a person who, though mentally ill, is harmless and can live safely outside an institution."

Dangerousness to self and/or grave disability as bases for commitment have received greater scrutiny with the increased prominence of homeless persons with mental illness. A much discussed case involved a woman in New York City who was forcibly removed from the street and admitted to a psychiatric ward on an emergency basis. A trial court granted her release based on contradictory medical reports as to her mental state, *In re Boggs,* No. 95656/87 (N.Y. Sup. Ct. Nov. 12, 1987), 12 MPDLR 14, but an appeals court reversed, finding clear and convincing evidence that Ms. Boggs had a mental illness and needed treatment to prevent serious harm to her well-being. *Boggs v. New York City Health & Hosps. Corp.,* 523 N.Y.S. 2d 71 (N.Y. App. Div. 1987), 12 MPDLR 238.

Periodic Review and Release

Most states limit the initial commitment period (often called emergency or observational commitment), after which a hearing must be held or the patient released. Periodic review ensures that patients do not remain hospitalized after they are no longer dangerous or in need of treatment. In addition, such review permits staff to consider and implement less restrictive alternatives. Continued confinement despite improved conditions may be statutorily and/or constitutionally invalid. For example, *Wyatt v. King,* 773 F. Supp. 1508 (M.D. Ala. 1991), 15 MPDLR 453, struck down Alabama's law that allowed persons with mental illness to be committed without periodic review. The court held that, pursuant to *Lynch v. Baxley,* 386 F. Supp. 378 (M.D. Ala. 1974), the state must conduct periodic court reviews that afford basic due process protections, including notice, the rights to attend the hearing and to counsel, and clear standards defining who can be committed.

Continued or extended commitment also is of limited duration, but usually is substantially longer than the initial period. Recommitment procedures generally are quite similar if not identical to the initial commitment proceedings — there must be a new petition, a new mental health evaluation, a new hearing, and the state has the burden of proof. *See Fasulo v. Arafeh,* 378 A.2d 553 (Conn. Sup. Ct. 1977), 2 MDLR 171.

While periodic review is a common practice, increasingly we also see the dilemma of the patient who is no longer dangerous to self or others but is not released due to the lack of satisfactory placement alternatives. The issue is whether the state has failed to meet its obligation to provide suitable community alternatives, or is acting reasonably in waiting for alternatives to become available. *See In re Commitment of S.L.*, 462 A.2d 1252 (N.J. Sup. Ct. 1983), 7 MDLR 378.

Outpatient and Preventive Commitment

Involuntary outpatient commitment (IOC) has emerged as a popular but controversial alternative to conventional court-ordered institutionalization. Every jurisdiction currently permits one or more general forms of IOC: conditional release; commitment to an outpatient program as a less restrictive alternative to hospitalization; and preventive commitment.

Most jurisdictions authorize conditional release, convalescent status, or provisional discharge to outpatient treatment after discharge from involuntary inpatient commitment. The common practice is to release the patient subject to certain conditions, after his/her condition improves during hospitalization. The former patient may be returned to the hospital if certain specified conditions are not met. Most courts have ruled, however, that a pre-revocation hearing must be held, at which the patient can try to show that he/she did not violate the release conditions. *See K.B. v. Sprenger,* No. 770292 (Minn. Dist. Ct., Hennepin County, Sept. 10, 1980), 5 MDLR 182; and *Hamel v. Brooks,* No. 78-115 (D. Or. Dec. 1979), 4 MDLR 97.

Most jurisdictions also allow or mandate outpatient commitment either as a less restrictive alternative to hospitalization or as a dispositional alternative for someone who meets the inpatient commitment criteria. For example, based on a statutory preference for less restrictive placements, the Rhode Island supreme court upheld outpatient treatment at a community mental health center for a man "whose continued unsupervised presence in the community would give rise to a likelihood of serious harm to himself or others." *Rhode Island Dep't of Mental Health, Retardation & Hosps. v. R.B.,* 549 A.2d 1028 (R.I. Sup. Ct. 1988), 13 MPDLR 89. An Indiana appeals court agreed that outpatients can be held in contempt of court for willfully refusing to take their medication. *See In re Tarpley*, 566 N.E.2d 71 (Ind. Ct. App. 1991), 15 MPDLR 216, and *In re Utley*, 565 N.E.2d 1153 (Ind. Ct. App. 1991), 15 MPDLR 217.

Preventive commitment generally applies a lower commitment standard than inpatient commitment. Outpatient treatment is compelled to avert a predicted deterioration of a person's mental health which, if left unchecked, would necessitate inpatient care. Commitment is based on a history of mental illness or present mental illness, rather than dangerousness, and the deprivation of liberty is justified by the patient's need for treatment, not the need to protect the individual or others from harm. Procedural protections are also less rigorous than under ordinary commitment provisions. As of 1990, only three states — North Carolina, Hawaii, Georgia — explicitly authorized preventive commitment. Each state applies a different commitment standard, but all provide that if the individual does not comply with the treatment program, the physician in charge may petition the court for inpatient hospitalization; the court must find that the person meets the inpatient commitment standard.

IOC has considerable support from family-oriented advocacy groups which see it as a way to provide some treatment and exercise control without the more drastic step of institutionalization. IOC also offers families and the state a means to intervene before the individual becomes dangerous. Critics of IOC voice a number of concerns, however, many of which center on the individual's liberties, the duty to find the least restrictive treatment environment, and the individual's right to refuse treatment. *See* Stefan, "Preventive Commitment: The Concept and Its Pitfalls," 11 MPDLR 288.

For a complete overview of outpatient commitment laws and legislative trends, *see* McCafferty & Dooley, "Involuntary Outpatient Commitment: An Update," 14 MPDLR 277, and Keilitz and Hall, "State Statutes Governing Involuntary Outpatient Civil Commitment," 9 MPDLR 378. *See also* Keilitz, "Empirical Studies of Involuntary Outpatient Commitment: Is It Working?" 14 MPDLR 368, for a review of research studies on the operation, patient characteristics, and effectiveness of IOC procedures and programs.

"Voluntary" and Third Party Commitment

"Voluntary" admission for mental health care generally refers to three types of admission procedures: informal; traditional, also called formal or conditional; and third party. Only the informal procedures, which allow patients to check themselves in and out with a minimum of paperwork and bureaucratic constraints, are truly voluntary. The traditional voluntary admission procedure departs from the informal scheme in the element of coercion that may precede an admission, and the limitations placed on release. The third party voluntary procedure really is a misnomer, since the person being admitted has not initiated the admission but is being committed upon someone else's request.

All jurisdictions except Alabama and Maine have enacted voluntary admission procedures. Some 10 states have voluntary procedures specifically denoted as informal, and four more have traditional procedures under which patients can check out with only minor administrative delay, as long as involuntary commitment procedures have not been initiated.

In *Zinermon v. Burch*, 494 U.S. 113 (1990), 14 MPDLR 116, the U.S. Supreme Court held that a §1983 action can be brought against state officials who commit someone "voluntarily" without obtaining informed consent. Since it was foreseeable that someone seeking voluntary admission for mental health treatment might be incompetent to give informed consent, anyone exercising reasonable professional judgment would have realized the need to review the person's competency to consent.

Juveniles, particularly those with parents or legal guardians, have less due process protections. In *Parham v. J.R.*, 442 U.S. 584 (1979), 3 MDLR 231, the U.S. Supreme Court held that an admitting physician's informal determination is sufficient for parents to commit their children to state hospitals. Later, the Eleventh Circuit held that once parents commit their minor child, there is no constitutional right to treatment in the least restrictive environment. *Doe v. Public Health Trust of Dade County*, 696 F.2d 901 (11th Cir. 1983), 7 MDLR 220. More recently, the Alabama supreme court extended *Parham* to private hospitalizations, ruling that parents have a common law right and duty to provide for their children's well-being and are presumed to act in their children's best interests. *R.J.D. v. Vaughan Clinic, P.C.*, 572 So. 2d 1225 (Ala. Sup. Ct. 1990), 15 MPDLR 217.

What is required to hold a voluntary patient? The Pennsylvania supreme court held that a voluntary patient who had agreed to short-term hospitalization could not then insist on a hearing or her release. *In re J.S.*, 586 A.2d 909 (Pa. Sup. Ct. 1991), 15 MPDLR 336. A New York court held that hospital officials cannot use a proceeding to transfer a voluntary patient to a state facility to also convert her to involuntary status. *In re Lesley*, 567 N.Y.S.2d 999 (N.Y. Sup. Ct. 1991), 15 MPDLR 336.

Criminal Mental Disability Issues

Civil-Criminal Dichotomy

Criminal trials differ significantly from civil commitment proceedings. (1) A criminal trial's purpose is to determine guilt or innocence and to punish persons found guilty; the purpose of civil commitment is to protect society and/or to provide necessary treatment. (2) The standard of proof in a criminal trial is beyond a reasonable doubt; civil commitment usually requires clear and convincing evidence. (3) Criminal confinement is limited to the sentence imposed; the duration of civil commitment is determined by the person's mental condition and how long he or she continues to meet the commitment standard.

Sometimes, however, criminal and civil elements are mixed, such as when a criminal defendant is incompetent to stand trial or is found not guilty by reason of insanity. The commitment and release proceedings in these contexts may be viewed as quasi-civil or something that is neither entirely criminal nor civil in nature.

Commitments through the criminal justice system generally occur when defendants found incompetent to stand trial or not guilty by reason of insanity are involuntarily hospitalized, defendants found guilty but mentally ill or convicted as mentally disordered sex offenders are given specialized mental health services in secure facilities in lieu of ordinary imprisonment, or a prison inmate who has a mental illness is transferred to a state hospital for treatment. If a transfer is involuntary, the prisoner must receive adequate notice, be represented by an advocate (not necessarily an attorney), and be allowed to present testimony and cross-examine witnesses. *Vitek v. Jones*, 445 U.S. 480 (1980), 4 MDLR 152.

For more information, *see* the American Bar Association's *Criminal Justice Mental Health Standards* published in 1984. The 102 "black letter" standards are published without commentary at 13 MPDLR 156.

Trial Competency

Incompetence to stand trial focuses on a defendant's present ability to understand the charges, the criminal process, and the potential punishment, and to assist in his or her defense. Due process is violated if a defendant is tried while incompetent. Thus, the court, defense counsel, and even the prosecutor, have an obligation to raise the incompetency issue whenever there is a bona fide doubt about the defendant's competence, *Pate v. Robinson*, 383 U.S. 375 (1966), or reasonable cause to believe the defendant is incompetent, *United States v. Bodey*, 547 F.2d 1383 (9th Cir. 1977), and *United States v. Nichelson*, 550 F.2d 502 (8th Cir. 1977).

Where a legitimate doubt is raised about the defendant's competency, the court will usually order the defendant evaluated pursuant to a temporary commitment order. Almost every state law specifies who must perform the evaluation; it usually must be a psychiatrist, but sometimes can be any physician or a clinical psychologist. The fifth amendment ban against compulsory self-incrimination often becomes an issue in these evaluations. Some jurisdictions, either by statute or court decision, make the defendant's statements during the exam inadmissible to prove guilt or to enhance the sentence, although other states provide that defendants who raise an issue about their trial competence waive their privilege against self-incrimination during the competency evaluation. Regardless of the state's approach, such statements generally are admissible to impeach the defendant's testimony. *See Estelle v. Smith*, 451 U.S. 454 (1981), 5 MDLR 231, and *Colorado v. Branch*, 805 P.2d 1075 (Colo. Sup. Ct. 1991), 15 MPDLR 338.

State laws vary as to which party has the burden of proof in incompetency proceedings. The U.S. Supreme Court recently held that California does not violate due process by requiring a defendant to prove incompetency by a preponderance of the evidence. *Medina v. California,* No. 90-8370 (U.S. Sup. Ct. June 22, 1992), *affirming,* 799 P.2d 1281 (Cal. Sup. Ct. 1990), 15 MPDLR 128. As long as the state satisfies due process by giving defendants access to procedures for making a competency evaluation, there is "no basis for holding that due process further requires the State to assume the burden of vindicating the defendant's constitutional right [not to be tried while legally incompetent] by persuading the trier of fact that the defendant is competent to stand trial."

Many state statutes adopted the trial competency test established by the Supreme Court in *Dusky v. United States,* 362 U.S. 402 (1960): "sufficient present ability to consult his lawyer with a reasonable degree of rational understanding and whether he has a rational as well as factual understanding of the proceedings against him."

A related issue is whether defendants have the right to refuse psychiatric medication that will make them competent. The Fourth Circuit upheld the forcible administration of medication to an incompetent and dangerous defendant where the decision was based on reasonable medical judgment. *United States v. Charters,* 863 F.2d 302 (4th Cir. 1988), 13 MPDLR 24, *cert. denied,* 494 U.S. 1016. *See also Washington v. Harper,* 494 U.S. 210 (1990), 14 MPDLR 124, in which the Supreme Court held that prisoners have only a limited right to refuse medication, and *Riggins v. Nevada,* 112 S. Ct. 1810 (1992), 16 MPDLR 268, in which the Court held that a pre-trial detainee has the right to refuse antipsychotic medication absent an overriding justification and determination of medical appropriateness. (*See* further discussion below on right to refuse medication.)

In the landmark decision *Jackson v. Indiana,* 406 U.S. 715 (1972), the U.S. Supreme Court approved commitment for the purpose of restoring a defendant to a level of functioning that allows the trial to continue. More importantly, the Court limited the duration of confinement by ruling that indeterminate commitment following a trial incompetency finding violates both federal due process and equal protection. Unless a formal civil commitment proceeding is initiated, a defendant found incompetent to stand trial cannot be detained longer than is reasonably necessary to restore the defendant's competency or to determine that restoration in the foreseeable future is unlikely.

Constitutionally, the permissible length of confinement is unresolved. States use various formulations, including indefinite hospitalization, subject to periodic review; no longer than the potential sentence upon conviction; and certain maximum periods, ranging from six months to three or more years. Courts often look to the reasonableness of the state's approach. *See, e.g., Yiadom v. Kiley,* 562 N.E.2d 310 (Ill. App. Ct. 1990), 15 MPDLR 132; *Illinois v. Christy,* 564 N.E.2d 238 (Ill. App. Ct. 1990), 15 MPDLR 223; and *Michigan v. Miller,* 463 N.W.2d 250 (Mich. Ct. App. 1990), 15 MPDLR 133.

Most states provide a formal procedure to inform the trial court that the defendant's competency has been restored. Commonly, a designated mental health official, the defendant, the prosecutor, or the court may initiate the restoration process. States generally entitle the defendant to a court hearing that focuses on the defendant's current fitness to proceed. If the defendant is found competent, the trial proceeds, the charges are dismissed, or civil commitment proceedings are initiated.

Other Criminal Competency Issues

Confessions

People in police custody have the right to remain silent, but anything they say after being informed of this right can be used against them. *See Miranda v. Arizona,* 384 U.S. 436 (1966). An individual may make a voluntary, knowing, and intelligent waiver of this right. The U.S. Supreme Court ruled, in *Colorado v. Connelly,* 479 U.S. 157 (1986), 11 MPDLR 19, that a defendant's mental condition does not, by itself, establish whether a confession was coerced or a waiver properly made. The defense must show either police coercion, or that the defendant was unable to make a knowing, intelligent waiver.

Subsequent cases have tried to refine *Connelly.* In *United States v. Bradshaw,* 935 F.2d 295 (D.C. Cir. 1991), 15 MPDLR 463, the court held that a separate inquiry must be made into whether the defendant had a "'full awareness both of the nature of the right being abandoned and the consequences of the decision to abandon it.'" *See also North Carolina v. Sanchez*, 400 S.E.2d 421 (N.C. Sup. Ct. 1991), 15 MPDLR 224; and *Illinois v. Bernasco*, 562 N.E.2d 958 (Ill. Sup. Ct. 1990), 15 MPDLR 135. The Ninth Circuit affirmed a waiver by a defendant with mental retardation who could not understand the waiver's consequences. "[S]uch a lack of foresight has never prevented an individual from waiving his Miranda rights." *Derrick v. Peterson*, 924 F.2d 813 (9th Cir. 1990), 15 MPDLR 225.

The Kansas supreme court noted that a confession is involuntary if a defendant is legally insane; otherwise, his or her mental condition is but one factor in determining voluntariness. *Kansas v. William*, 807 P.2d 1292 (Kan. Sup. Ct. 1991), 15 MPDLR 347.

Pleas

As with confessions, pleas must be made knowingly and voluntarily, i.e., a defendant must have the mental capacity to understand the rights he or she is foregoing by entering a plea and the consequences of his or her choice. *See, e.g., Tiller v. Esposito*, 911 F.2d 575 (11th Cir. 1990), 15 MPDLR 30; *Chichackly v. United States*, 926 F.2d 624 (7th Cir. 1991), 15 MPDLR 556; *Long v. Iowa*, 920 F.2d 4 (8th Cir. 1990), 15 MPDLR 138; *New Hampshire v. Sarette*, 589 A.2d 125 (N.H. Sup. Ct. 1991), 15 MPDLR 346; *United States v. Haga*, 931 F.2d 642 (10th Cir. 1991), 15 MPDLR 346; and *United States ex rel. Butler v. Bara*, 757 F. Supp. 210 (N.D.N.Y. 1990), 15 MPDLR 347.

Sentencing/Death Penalty

The Supreme Court has held that a defendant must be able to understand that a sentence is being imposed and why he or she is going to receive that punishment. *Ford v. Wainwright*, 477 U.S. 399 (1986), 10 MPDLR 278. Without such an understanding, a sentence will serve no retributive purpose, an argument that is particularly compelling in death penalty cases. *See, e.g., Cuevas v. Collins*, 932 F.2d 1078 (5th Cir. 1991), 15 MPDLR 464; and *Rector v. Clark*, 923 F.2d 570 (8th Cir. 1991), 15 MPDLR 227.

A defendant's mental impairment may also play a role in

determining an appropriate sentence. On the federal level, this often involves the court's decision whether to impose a sentence below that authorized by the sentencing guidelines. *See, e.g., United States v. Ruklick,* 919 F.2d 95 (8th Cir. 1991), 15 MPDLR 361; *United States v. Gentry,* 925 F.2d 186 (7th Cir. 1991), 15 MPDLR 245; *United States v. Fonner,* 920 F.2d 1330 (7th Cir. 1990), 15 MPDLR 245; and *United States v. Poff,* 926 F.2d 588 (7th Cir. 1991), 15 MPDLR 363.

The U.S. Supreme Court ruled that the trier of fact must be allowed to consider a defendant's mental impairment as a mitigating factor. *Penry v. Lynaugh,* 492 U.S. 302 (1989), 13 MPDLR 334, reversed and remanded a death sentence because the trial court did not instruct the jury to consider the defendant's mental retardation. The Court also ruled, however, that the eighth amendment's prohibition against cruel and unusual punishment did not automatically bar the execution of people with mental retardation. In contrast, the Georgia supreme court has held that the execution of people with mental retardation violates the state constitution. *Fleming v. Zant,* 386 S.E.2d 339 (Ga. Sup. Ct. 1989), 14 MPDLR 132. Note also, that the federal Controlled Substances Act, 21 U.S.C. §848(l), and laws in Georgia, Maryland, Kentucky, New Mexico, and Tennessee bar the execution of persons with mental retardation.

In another important death penalty case, *Estelle v. Smith,* 451 U.S. 454 (1981), 5 MDLR 231, the U.S. Supreme Court held that a psychiatrist cannot use a trial competency evaluation to find that a defendant poses a future danger and thus deserves an "enhanced" sentence, without warning the defendant beforehand how the evaluation will be used. While the Court expressed skepticism about a clinician's ability to predict future dangerousness, it noted that the factfinder has to determine the proper weight to give such testimony.

In *Barefoot v. Estelle,* 463 U.S. 880 (1983), 7 MDLR 303, the Court ruled that at capital sentencing hearings, psychiatrists may predict a defendant's potential future dangerousness, even using hypothetical questions about the probability of future crimes. In *Satterwhite v. Texas,* 486 U.S. 249 (1988), 12 MPDLR 340, however, the Court ruled that defense counsel must be given proper notice before a psychiatric exam on future dangerousness is given during the sentencing phase of a capital case. Absent such notice, it is reversible error to admit psychiatric testimony, unless it is shown beyond a reasonable doubt that the testimony did not contribute to the sentence.

Victims/Witnesses

Mental capacity may be an issue for crime victims or witnesses. With victims, the issue often involves the capacity of someone with mental retardation to consent to a sexual act. *See, e.g., New Jersey v. Olivio,* 589 A.2d 597 (N.J. Sup. Ct. 1991), 15 MPDLR 345; *Idaho v. Soura,* 796 P.2d 109 (Idaho Sup. Ct. 1990), 15 MPDLR 29; and *Ortiz v. Texas,* 804 S.W.2d 177 (Tex. Ct. App. 1991), 15 MPDLR 349. With witnesses, the issue is whether they have the ability to tell the truth, and to perceive, recall, and tell about the events in question. *See, e.g., United States v. Pryce,* 938 F.2d 1343 (D.C. Cir. 1991), 15 MPDLR 558; *Bussey v. Kentucky,* 797 S.W.2d 483 (Ky. Sup. Ct. 1990), 15 MPDLR 137; *West Virginia v. Merritt,* 396 S.E.2d 871 (W. Va. Sup. Ct. 1990), 15 MPDLR 31; *Rhode Island v. Lopez,* 583 A.2d 529 (R.I. Sup. Ct. 1990), 15 MPDLR 226; *United States v. Devin,* 918 F.2d 280 (1st Cir. 1990), 15 MPDLR 137; and *United States v. Moore,* 923 F.2d 910 (1st Cir. 1991), 15 MPDLR 226.

Insanity Defense

Individuals who do not have the mental capacity to be criminally responsible for their actions cannot be convicted and may be found not guilty by reason of insanity (NGRI). While insanity acquittees cannot be punished, they almost always will be confined in a secure treatment facility based on their dangerous acts and mental disability.

The first and, due to recent changes, the most prominent insanity defense formulation is the M'Naghten Rule. The defendant must show that "at the time of the committing of the act, the party accused was labouring under such a defect of reason, from disease of the mind, as not to know the nature and quality of the act he was doing; or, if he did know it, that he did not know he was doing what was wrong." At one time, an overwhelming majority of jurisdictions used this or a close version of this test; today, about half the states use it. In addition, courts have fine-tuned the definition, such as stating that an inability to distinguish right from wrong requires not only that a defendant not know that his act is illegal, but also that it is wrong according to a societal standard of moral wrong. *See Colorado v. Serravo,* 823 P.2d 128 (Colo. Sup. Ct. 1992), 16 MPDLR 271; and *New Jersey v. Worlock,* 569 A.2d 1314 (N.J. Sup. Ct. 1990), 14 MPDLR 392.

After M'Naghten, a number of variations of the insanity defense developed, including the "irresistible impulse test," *see Smith v. United States,* 36 F.2d 548 (D.C. Cir. 1929), which added an excuse for acts committed under overwhelming compulsions that are a product of a mental disease; and the "product of mental disease or mental defect test," *see Durham v. United States,* 214 F.2d 862 (D.C. Cir. 1954).

In the 1950s, the American Law Institute devised what for some time became the most popular insanity test: "a person is not responsible for criminal conduct if at the time of such conduct as a result of mental disease or defect he lacks substantial capacity either to appreciate the criminality of his conduct or to conform his conduct to the requirements of law." The test specifically excludes "an abnormality manifested only by repeated criminal or otherwise anti-social conduct." While approximately half the jurisdictions used this standard, several states dropped it in the 1980s, reacting to the Hinckley decision and growing concern about the premature release of dangerous insanity acquittees.

Several proposals changed the insanity defense formulation: a complementary verdict of "guilty but mentally ill" (GBMI), in which a mental impairment affects the defendant's capacity at the time of the crime, but not to the degree needed to establish insanity, *see* discussion below; and a provision that eliminates the insanity defense, to the extent permitted by the U.S. Constitution, without substituting an alternative.

The American Bar Association, at its February 1983 mid-year meeting, adopted a variation of M'Naghten "which focuses solely on whether the defendant, as a result of mental disease or defect, was unable to appreciate the wrongfulness of that defendant's conduct at the time of the offense charged." The ABA also opposed the guilty but mentally ill alternative and any efforts to abolish the insanity defense.

Rather than actually abolishing the insanity defense, most post-Hinckley changes focused on the burden and standard of proof, and an acquittee's commitment and release. In Idaho, however, the state supreme court upheld the constitutionality of a state law which mandated that a "'[m]ental condition shall not be a defense to any charge of criminal conduct.'" *Idaho v. Searcy*, 798 P.2d 914 (Idaho Sup. Ct. 1990), 14 MPDLR 485. Idaho law allows evidence of the defendant's mental ability to form the necessary criminal intent, but bars the use of such evidence as an affirmative insanity defense. *See also Idaho v. Rhoades*, 820 P.2d 665 (Idaho Sup. Ct. 1991), 16 MPDLR 144. The Montana supreme court approved a similar formulation. *See Montana v. Korell*, 690 P.2d 992 (Mont. Sup. Ct. 1984), 9 MPDLR 91.

Burden & Standard of Proof

A defendant is presumed sane and, in most jurisdictions, must plead NGRI as an affirmative defense. Before a court will allow defendants to pursue the defense, they must present sufficient evidence to establish a reasonable basis for the plea. In the 1970s, all federal courts and approximately half the states required that once the defense met that initial burden, the prosecution had to prove the defendant was sane. In the 1980s, however, the trend changed to require that the defendant prove insanity, and while most jurisdictions require proof by a preponderance of the evidence, the U.S. Supreme Court has held that a state does not violate the constitution by imposing a burden on the defendant of proof beyond a reasonable doubt. *See Leland v. Oregon*, 343 U.S. 790 (1952), and *Martin v. Ohio*, 480 U.S. 228 (1987). Today, the Insanity Defense Reform Act, 18 U.S.C. §17 (1988), places the burden on defendants in federal court, and approximately two-third of the states follow that approach. Federal defendants must prove insanity by clear and convincing evidence. Where the prosecution still has the burden of proof, it generally must prove the defendant sane beyond a reasonable doubt.

Satisfying the applicable standard frequently becomes a "battle of the experts," with the court or jury determining the credibility of the witnesses. In general, lay witness testimony can support a finding of sanity or insanity, even in the face of contrary expert testimony, as long as the witness had a sufficient opportunity to observe the defendant in close proximity to the time of the crime and to form an opinion as to his or her sanity. *See, e.g., Kansas v. Baker*, 819 P.2d 1173 (Kan. Sup. Ct. 1991), 16 MPDLR 148; *Ex parte Milteer*, 571 So. 2d 998 (Ala. Sup. Ct. 1990), 15 MPDLR 238; and *Billotti v. Dodrill*, 394 S.E.2d 32 (W. Va. Sup. Ct. 1990), 14 MPDLR 490.

Dispositions

Insanity acquittees are subject to formal civil commitment proceedings, receive a hearing on their current dangerousness, or are committed because their otherwise criminal behavior shows they pose a danger. The U.S. Supreme Court recently struck down a Louisiana statute permitting the continued confinement of an insanity acquittee who no longer had a mental illness but who could not prove he was no longer dangerous. *Foucha v. Louisiana*, 112 S. Ct. 1780 (1992), 16 MPDLR 266.

Previously, the High Court had ruled that an insanity acquittee may be detained for longer than the maximum possible sentence after a conviction, *Jones v. United States*, 463 U.S. 354 (1983), 7 MDLR 299, and upheld the preponderance of the evidence standard for the indefinite commitment of insanity acquittees, a lower standard than is applied to civil commitment. The Court found a rational basis for treating these two classes of persons differently, because insanity acquittees have been found, by proof beyond a reasonable doubt, to have committed an act that would have been a crime had they been sane. Also, since treatment, not punishment, is the basis for an acquittee's commitment, the length of his potential sentence is irrelevant to the appropriate period of confinement.

Some jurisdictions do limit the commitment period to the maximum potential sentence upon conviction, after which the person can be detained only if he meets the civil commitment criteria. Moreover, state statutes generally entitle acquittees to periodic exams to ensure that they still require commitment, and allow them to petition for release at any time. The Insanity Defense Reform Act of 1984, which provides insanity acquittees with medical reassessments rather than adversarial commitment hearings, withstood a due process and equal protection challenge. *United States v. LaFromboise*, 836 F.2d 1149 (8th Cir. 1988), 12 MPDLR 243.

Guilty But Mentally Ill

At least 13 states (Alaska, Delaware, Georgia, Illinois, Indiana, Kentucky, Michigan, Montana, New Mexico, Pennsylvania, South Carolina, South Dakota, and Utah) recognize the guilty but mentally ill (GBMI) alternative to an insanity finding. The state must prove beyond a reasonable doubt that the defendant committed the act charged. Also, the defendant must have had a mental illness, but not been legally insane, at the time of the crime. As with the insanity defense, this determination often becomes a battle of the experts.

While the GBMI verdict is based on a need for treatment, not all state laws require treatment and even when they do, treatment may not be guaranteed. The New Mexico supreme court held that the state law's failure to require treatment did not violate due process or equal protection; the GBMI verdict fulfills a legitimate state purpose, and the state can rationally treat defendants with mental illnesses differently depending on whether they are criminally culpable. *New Mexico v. Neely,* 819 P.2d 249 (N.M. Sup. Ct. 1991), 16 MPDLR 146. In addition, a court may find that treatment is inappropriate, *Utah v. Anderson,* 797 P.2d 416 (Utah Sup. Ct. 1990), 15 MPDLR 40; aggravating factors may outweigh mitigating factors and justify an enhanced sentence, *Wall v. Indiana,* 573 N.E.2d 890 (Ind. Sup. Ct. 1991), 15 MPDLR 474; or the death penalty may be imposed despite a statutory treatment requirement, *Harris v. Indiana,* 499 N.E.2d 723 (Ind. Sup. Ct. 1986), 11 MPDLR 93, *cert. denied,* 482 U.S. 909 (1987). *See also South Carolina v. Wilson,* 413 S.E.2d 19 (S.C. Sup. Ct. 1992), 16 MPDLR 145.

Diminished Capacity

Diminished capacity does not eliminate criminal responsibility, but recognizes mental illness as a mitigating factor in certain situations. Thus, regardless of whether a defendant raises an insanity defense, psychiatric evidence may be admissible to show that the defendant could not form the specific intent needed to commit the crime. *See, e.g., New Jersey v. Breakiron,* 532 A.2d 199 (N.J. Sup. Ct. 1987), 12 MPDLR 140, and *Kansas v. Hill,* 744 P.2d 1228 (Kan. Sup. Ct. 1987), 12 MPDLR 140. A defendant need not prove that his or her diminished capacity negated criminal culpability, however, since the state must prove each element of the crime, including that the defendant acted knowingly and purposefully. *See, e.g., New Jersey v. Moore,* 585 A.2d 864 (N.J. Sup. Ct. 1991), 15 MPDLR 228; and *New Jersey v. Oglesby,* 585 A.2d 916 (N.J. Sup. Ct. 1991), 15 MPDLR 229.

The Ninth Circuit held that the Insanity Defense Reform Act of 1984, 18 U.S.C. §17, did not abolish the diminished capacity defense. *United States v. Twine,* 853 F.2d 676 (9th Cir. 1988), 12 MPDLR 505.

Mentally Disordered Sex Offenders (MDSO)

Approximately 14 jurisdictions have laws, variously referred to as "sexually dangerous person acts," "mentally disordered sex offender acts," and "sexual psychopath laws," targeted at people with propensities to commit sex offenses. The laws generally require that the defendant plead guilty to or be convicted of a sex crime, and that his criminal behavior be habitual and beyond his control. The purpose of these laws is to treat the offender and protect society. While some statutes continue to permit an indeterminate commitment, others provide for commitment or imprisonment limited to the maximum potential sentence for a conviction. Release generally requires a medical finding that the person has recovered, at least to the extent that he no longer poses a danger to others.

While states must provide certain fundamental protections, such as the rights to an attorney, to be heard, and to present and confront witnesses, *see Specht v. Patterson,* 386 U.S. 605 (1967), other protections, such as an independent psychiatrist to assist in a recovery proceeding, may not apply. *See, e.g., Illinois v. Finkle,* 573 N.E.2d 381 (Ill. App. Ct. 1991), 15 MPDLR 472.

While courts generally require proof beyond a reasonable doubt, *see, e.g., Illinois v. Pembrock,* 342 N.E.2d 28 (Ill. Sup. Ct. 1976),

1 MDLR 15, and *United States ex rel. Stachulak v. Coughlin*, 520 F.2d 931 (7th Cir. 1975), the Nebraska supreme court ruled that only clear and convincing evidence, the civil commitment standard, is necessary. *Nebraska v. Harris*, 463 N.W.2d 829 (Neb. Sup. Ct. 1990), 15 MPDLR 240.

Finally, sex offenders who are placed on probation may be compelled to complete a counseling program, *Utah v. Hodges*, 798 P.2d 270 (Utah Ct. App. 1990), 15 MPDLR 42, and to obey the program's requirements, such as admitting guilt. *Vermont v. Mace*, 578 A.2d 104 (Vt. Sup. Ct. 1990), 15 MPDLR 43.

Expert Assistance

In *Ake v. Oklahoma*, 470 U.S. 68 (1985), 9 MPDLR 97, the U.S. Supreme Court determined that an indigent defendant has the right to competent, independent psychiatric assistance in at least two circumstances: (1) when the defendant shows that his or her sanity is likely to be a significant issue at trial; and (2) in a capital sentencing proceeding when the prosecution raises the issue of the defendant's future dangerousness. Courts have ruled that *Ake* requires a defendant to show a reasonable probability that an expert will assist the defense and that a denial of such assistance will result in fundamental unfairness. *See, e.g., Moore v. Kemp*, 809 F.2d 702 (11th Cir. 1987), *cert. denied*, 481 U.S. 1054 (1987); *North Carolina v. Lloyd*, 364 S.E.2d 316 (N.C. Sup. Ct. 1988), 12 MPDLR 246; *Ohio v. Powell*, 552 N.E.2d 191 (Ohio Sup. Ct. 1990), 14 MPDLR 307; and *Christenson v. Georgia*, 402 S.E.2d 41 (Ga. Sup. Ct. 1991), 15 MPDLR 364.

Courts also have held that *Ake* entitles defendants to a qualified, independent psychiatrist to assist in whatever capacity defense counsel deems appropriate, including exploring the basis for and advisability of an insanity defense, testifying at trial, and aiding in the cross-examination of adverse witnesses. *Blake v. Kemp*, 758 F.2d 523 (11th Cir. 1985), 9 MPDLR 257, *cert. denied*, 474 U.S. 998 (1985), 9 MPDLR 408; *Smith v. McCormick*, 914 F.2d 1153 (9th Cir. 1990), 15 MPDLR 47; and *Cowley v. Stricklin*, 929 F.2d 640 (11th Cir. 1991), 15 MPDLR 363. The Eleventh Circuit ruled that due process entitled a defendant who alleged a delusional compulsion to a third psychiatric evaluation, where two examining psychiatrists had not actually evaluated his mental state at the time of the crime. *Ford v. Gaither*, 953 F.2d 1296 (11th Cir. 1992), 16 MPDLR 275.

Ake does not entitle the defendant to the appointment of a psychiatrist of his or her choice, or to a favorable psychiatric opinion, *Martin v. Wainwright*, 770 F.2d 918 (11th Cir. 1985), 9 MPDLR 419, *cert. denied*, 479 U.S. 909 (1986), *Henderson v. Dugger*, 925 F.2d 1309 (11th Cir. 1991), 15 MPDLR 232, and defendants may not raise a constitutional challenge to the competency of state-funded assistance. *Harris v. Vasquez*, 949 F.2d 1497 (9th Cir. 1991), 16 MPDLR 159, *amending* 943 F.2d 930 (9th Cir. 1991), 16 MPDLR 41, and 913 F.2d 606 (9th Cir. 1990), 15 MPDLR 34.

Courts differ as to whether *Ake* applies when the defendant has not pled insanity. While *Little v. Armontrout*, 835 F.2d 1240 (8th Cir. 1987), *cert. denied*, 487 U.S. 1210 (1988), held that the decision should rest on the importance of the scientific issue, the Sixth Circuit held that a state-funded psychiatrist need not be provided when a capital murder defendant raises a diminished capacity defense, *Kordenbrock v. Scroggy*, 919 F.2d 1091 (6th Cir. 1990), 15 MPDLR 246. The Tenth Circuit held, in *Liles v. Saffle*, 945 F.2d 333 (10th Cir. 1991), *cert. denied, Saffle v. Liles*, 112 S. Ct. 956, 16 MPDLR 28, that a trial court violated due process in denying state-funded psychiatric assistance to a defendant who had not pled insanity. The defendant's mental health history, treatment, and conflicting findings as to his trial competency established that he could have made a threshold showing that his sanity would be significant to his defense, and one of the functions of a court-appointed expert is to assist in evaluating the viability of an insanity defense.

Rights Within the Institution

Institutional conditions have been a major area of mental disability litigation. The rights to treatment/habilitation, to the basic necessities of life, to refuse treatment, and to treatment in the least restrictive environment, have gained various degrees of recognition.

Statutory Rights

In 1980, Congress enacted the Civil Rights of Institutionalized Persons Act (CRIPA), 42 U.S.C. §1997 et seq., which authorized the U.S. Department of Justice to sue to enforce state institution residents' federal constitutional and statutory rights. Despite this law, however, serious rights abuses persisted, due largely to inadequate staffing and resources and poor training. Moreover, a federal appeals court held that an institution's employees did not have a private right of action under CRIPA, since the law was aimed at protecting residents, and employees were not members of the class "for whose special benefit the statute was enacted." *Price v. Brittain*, 874 F.2d 252 (5th Cir. 1989), 13 MPDLR 471.

Congress subsequently created a protection and advocacy system for persons with mental illness similar to the system already in existence for persons with developmental disabilities, designed primarily to address the problems of institutionalized persons with mental illnesses. *See* Protection and Advocacy for Mentally Ill Individuals Act of 1986, 42 U.S.C. §10801 et seq. (1988). A federal court held, however, that the Patient Bill of Rights provisions of the act did not create any judicially enforceable rights or duties or a private right of action. *Brooks v. Johnson & Johnson, Inc.*, 685 F. Supp. 107 (E.D. Pa. 1988), 12 MPDLR 466. *See also Pennhurst State School & Hosp. v. Halderman*, 451 U.S. 1 (1981) 5 MDLR 162, which made a similar ruling with respect to the Developmentally Disabled Assistance and Bill of Rights Act of 1975, 42 U.S.C. §6010.

Constitutional Rights

Wyatt v. Stickney, 325 F. Supp. 781 (M.D. Ala. 1971), and 344 F. Supp. 373 (M.D. Ala. 1972), *aff'd sub nom.*, *Wyatt v. Aderholt*, 503 F.2d 1305 (5th Cir. 1974), held that patients with mental disabilities have a constitutional right to treatment, or to "habilitation." If these patients did not have an opportunity to receive treatment, they were no longer patients, but merely residents with indefinite sentences. Subsequently, the court set minimal constitutional treatment and habilitation standards. For more recent developments in this litigation, *see* 15 MPDLR 249 and 368.

In *Donaldson v. O'Connor*, 493 F.2d 507 (5th Cir. 1974), the Fifth Circuit held that people facing the extreme loss of liberty that results from civil commitment have a due process right to minimally adequate treatment. In *O'Connor v. Donaldson*, 422 U.S. 563 (1975), 1 MDLR 336, the High Court did not, and has yet to, endorse a constitutional right to treatment. The Supreme Court did find that involuntarily committed patients are entitled to release if they: (1) are being warehoused in the institution; (2) do not present a danger to themselves or others; and (3) are capable of living in the community with the help of friends or relatives.

Donaldson laid the basis for nondangerous mental patients to assert their rights to less restrictive alternative dispositions or minimal care and treatment while hospitalized. In examining the issue of competency to give informed consent to voluntary commitment, the Supreme Court expanded *Donaldson*, stating that the constitution does not permit the civil commitment of someone with a mental illness who is not dangerous and can live safely outside an institution. *Zinermon v. Burch*, 494 U.S. 113 (1990), 14 MPDLR 116.

Youngberg v. Romeo, 457 U.S. 307 (1982), 6 MDLR 223, is a landmark decision establishing minimal civil rights of persons in state mental institutions. While avoiding a right to treatment, the Supreme Court held that state facility residents have a constitutional right to the basic necessities of life, reasonably safe living conditions, freedom from undue restraint, and the minimally adequate training needed to enhance or further their ability to exercise other constitutional rights.

Youngberg also established the reasonable exercise of professional judgment as the standard to determine whether a state agent has violated a resident's constitutional rights. Patients are allowed to present evidence to overcome the presumption that reasonable judgment has been exercised. State and federal appellate courts applying the basic principles established in *Youngberg* and its progeny have shown a great deal of deference to the judgments of mental health professionals, and have overturned trial court decisions that second-guessed properly exercised professional judgments. Thus, residents with mental retardation have a constitutional right to habilitation in accordance with the prevailing standard of practice, not necessarily to habilitation in a community placement. *S.H. v. Edwards*, 860 F.2d 1045 (11th Cir. 1988), 13 MPDLR 105. See also *Buckner v. United States*, No. 88-2003-OG (D.D.C. July 26, 1989), 14 MPDLR 345; *Society for Good Will to Retarded Children, Inc. v. Cuomo*, 902 F.2d 1085 (2d Cir. 1990), 14 MPDLR 315, and 745 F. Supp. 879 (E.D.N.Y. 1990), 15 MPDLR 145; *Dixon ARC v. Thompson*, 440 N.E.2d 117 (Ill. Sup. Ct. 1982), 6 MDLR 303; and *New York ARC v. Carey*, 706 F.2d 956 (2d Cir. 1983), 7 MDLR 226.

Courts have, however, taken appropriate action when the state, through its administrators and employees, has not met reasonable levels of professional competency in carrying out constitutional and statutory mandates. For example, in *ARC of North Dakota v. Olson*, 561 F. Supp. 473 (D.N.D. 1982), 6 MDLR 374, *aff'd*, 713 F.2d 1384 (8th Cir. 1983), 7 MDLR 465, the court required training that would allow residents to retain the minimum self-care skills they had when they were institutionalized. Also, in *Thomas S. v. Flaherty*, 902 F.2d 250 (4th Cir. 1990), 14 MPDLR 315, the Fourth Circuit held that adults with mental retardation in North Carolina's psychiatric hospitals were entitled to community placements based on treating professionals' case-by-case findings that such placements were necessary. See also *Jackson v. Fort Stanton Hosp. & Training School*, 757 F. Supp. 1243 (D.N.M. 1990), 15 MPDLR 248; *Woe v. Cuomo*, 729 F.2d 96 (2d Cir. 1984), 8 MPDLR 280, *cert. denied*, 469 U.S. 936 (1984); and *Scott v. Plante*, 691 F.2d 634 (3d Cir. 1982), 7 MDLR 74.

Least Restrictive Environment

The doctrine of the least restrictive environment provides that restrictions on liberty should be limited to the minimum necessary to accomplish the asserted government purpose. This is a key concept used to support placements in smaller, more home-like facilities. Such placements are aimed at improving the residents' quality of life and increasing their chance of maximizing their independence. The principle also serves as the basis for limiting the use of intrusive treatments and therapies within an institution, particularly the use of psychotropic medication, seclusion, and restraint.

Wyatt v. Stickney, supra, at p. 41, applied the least restrictive alternative principle to residents with mental retardation and those with mental illness. The court required that an institution attempt to move residents to less restrictive settings, less structured units, smaller facilities or units, integrated community placements, and independent placements, as appropriate.

In *Caswell v. Secretary of Health & Human Servs.,* No. 77-0488-CV-W-8 (W.D. Mo. Feb. 8, 1983), 7 MDLR 221, a consent decree indicated how the right to the least restrictive environment leads to deinstitutionalization and normalization. Once it was agreed that residents of a large institution were entitled to treatment in the least restrictive appropriate setting, a plan was devised to provide a uniform system for clinical patient reviews, individualized treatment plans, and referrals for community placement.

Treatment Refusals

It is well-established that competent persons have the right to refuse psychiatric medication. In 1990, the U.S. Supreme Court held that all persons, including convicted prisoners, have a due process interest in refusing such medications. *Washington v. Harper,* 494 U.S. 210 (1990), 14 MPDLR 124. In prisons, however, these drugs may be forcibly administered if the majority of an independent administrative review panel agrees with the treating physician that the prisoner has a serious mental illness, is dangerous to self or others (or is gravely disabled), and the proposed treatment is in the prisoner's best interest. *See Riggins v. Nevada, supra,* at p. 29, concerning the rights of pre-trial detainees.

As to defendants committed as incompetent to stand trial, the Fourth Circuit deferred to the reasonable professional judgment of medical personnel in finding that, consistent with due process, antipsychotic medication can be forcibly administered. *United States v. Charters,* 863 F.2d 302 (4th Cir. 1988), 13 MPDLR 24, *cert. denied,* 494 U.S. 1016 (1990).

The question of the right to refuse medication has yet to be answered definitively in the civil context, and a conflict persists over this issue, particularly between the legal and medical professions. Moreover, while courts have consistently ruled that patient autonomy is an important if not overriding factor, court decisions are not uniform.

The due process hearing model was first articulated in what has become known as the *Rogers* litigation. The U.S. Supreme Court refused to decide if there was a constitutional right to decide whether to be treated with antipsychotic medication, and remanded a First Circuit decision recognizing such a right. *See Mills v. Rogers,* 457 U.S. 291 (1982), 6 MDLR 221, *remanding, Rogers v. Okin,* 634 F.2d 650 (1st Cir. 1980), 5 MDLR 17. Massachusetts' highest court was asked to review the issue under state law, which led to a decision that involuntarily committed patients who have not been adjudicated incompetent have a right to refuse antipsychotic medication in a nonemergency situation. Incompetent patients have a similar right, but it must be exercised through a court-approved substituted judgment treatment plan. *Rogers v. Commissioner of the Dep't of Mental Health,* 458 N.E.2d 308 (Mass. Sup. Jud. Ct. 1983), 8 MPDLR 103.

The Colorado supreme court established the most far-reaching due process hearing approach. In *Colorado v. Medina,* 705 P.2d 961 (Colo. Sup. Ct. 1985), 9 MPDLR 426, the court held that an adversarial hearing is required before antipsychotic drugs may be administered in a nonemergency. Clear and convincing evidence must show that (1) the patient is incompetent; (2) treatment is necessary to prevent the likelihood of harm to self or others or significant long-term deterioration of the patient's mental condition; (3) a less intrusive treatment is not available; and (4) the need for treatment is compelling enough to override any legitimate interest in refusing it.

Applying a right to privacy under the state constitution, the Minnesota supreme court held that involuntary patients are entitled to a hearing before being given neuroleptics. Moreover, state officials will not be immune from liability if they fail to secure court approval before administering such medication. *Jarvis v. Levine,* 418 N.W.2d 139 (Minn. Sup. Ct. 1988), 12 MPDLR 144. Likewise, a California appeals court held that absent a judicial incompetency determination, patients have a right under state law to refuse antipsychotic medications in nonemergencies. *Riese v. St. Mary's Hosp. & Medical Center,* 243 Cal. Rptr. 241 (Cal. Ct. App. 1987),

12 MPDLR 145, 255. And, the Wisconsin supreme court ruled, on equal protection grounds, that the state has no power to forcibly administer psychotropic medication in nonemergency situations to patients who have not been adjudged incompetent. *Wisconsin ex rel. Jones v. Gerhardstein,* 416 N.W.2d 883 (Wis. Sup. Ct. 1987), 12 MPDLR 31. See also *Bee v. Greaves,* 744 F.2d 1387 (10th Cir. 1984), 9 MPDLR 25, and *Keyhea v. Rushen,* No. 67432 (Cal. Super. Ct. Oct. 31, 1986), 11 MPDLR 24.

Other courts have articulated due process approaches that do not embrace direct judicial review, depending more on administrative procedures. In *Rennie v. Klein,* 720 F.2d 266 (3d Cir. 1983), 8 MPDLR 18, the Third Circuit reviewed New Jersey's three-step internal administrative process in which a facility's medical director or a designee had the final decisionmaking authority. The court held that involuntarily committed patients have a right to refuse antipsychotic medication, as long as their exercise of this right does not endanger them or others.

Similarly, the Second Circuit approved New York's approach, ruling that antipsychotic medication can be administered involuntarily, even though commitment does not require a finding of dangerousness, as long as the treating physician's decision has received three levels of medical review and the patient had access to counsel throughout the proceedings. *Project Release v. Prevost,* 722 F.2d 960 (2d Cir. 1983), 8 MPDLR 86. New York's highest court nevertheless found that even those procedures did not satisfy the state constitution's higher standards which, in nonemergency situations, require a separate court determination that patients were incompetent to make treatment decisions. *Rivers v. Katz,* 495 N.E.2d 337 (N.Y. Ct. App. 1986), 10 MPDLR 284.

Finally, Maryland's highest court held that while state law satisfied an insanity acquittee's substantive due process right to refuse antipsychotic medication, the state scheme did not meet *Harper's* procedural due process requirements. These procedural deficiencies invalidated the entire statutory scheme, meaning that state common law principles applied to prohibit "the non-consensual administration of drugs to a mentally competent adult under non-emergency circumstances." *Williams v. Wilzack,* 573 A.2d 809 (Md. Ct. App. 1990), 14 MPDLR 317.

Deinstitutionalization

Despite the struggle for rights within institutions, many people consider large facilities an undesirable way to provide treatment/habilitation to people with mental disabilities. The deinstitutionalization movement matured in the 1970s, as the media began focusing on the horrors and inadequacies of many mental institutions, which often had become human warehouses.

Supporters of deinstitutionalization used a variety of means, including legislatures and the media, to encourage and compel society to develop the knowledge, skill, resources, and motivation to serve individuals with mental disabilities in the most natural environments possible. It was only through the courts, however, that deinstitutionalization became focused.

Constitutional Rights

O'Connor v. Donaldson, 422 U.S. 563 (1975), 1 MDLR 336, was the first key deinstitutionalization case. This Supreme Court decision led to the release of a patient who did not pose a danger to himself or others, and who had resources in the community upon which he could rely. This set the stage for a second generation of cases, most notably represented by more than 15 years of litigation in *Halderman v. Pennhurst State School & Hosp.,* involving a large, not atypical, institution in Pennsylvania. *See* 446 F. Supp. 1295 (E.D. Pa. 1977), 2 MDLR 201, 3 MDLR 238; *modified,* 612 F.2d 84 (3d Cir. 1979), 4 MDLR 14; *rev'd, Pennhurst v. Halderman,* 451 U.S. 1 (1981), 5 MDLR 162; *aff'd prior judgment, Halderman v. Pennhurst,* 673 F.2d 647 (3d Cir. 1982), 6 MDLR 70; *rev'd and remanded, Pennhurst v. Halderman,* 465 U.S. 89 (1984), 8 MPDLR 7 (Pennhurst II). *See also* 9 MPDLR 427, 13 MPDLR 436, 14 MPDLR 182, 14 MPDLR 226, and 16 MPDLR 285.

In *Pennhurst,* the district court held that people with mental retardation, voluntarily or involuntarily institutionalized at Pennsylvania's state hospital, had a federal constitutional right to be provided with "minimally adequate habilitation" in the "least restrictive environment." Since large institutions could not provide the required habilitation, the court ordered the institution closed and the residents moved to suitable "community living arrangements" where they were more likely to receive adequate habilitation. The Third Circuit affirmed on federal statutory grounds.

The United States Supreme Court overruled the Third Circuit, holding that state recipients of federal funds under the Developmental Disabilities Act were not obligated to provide habilitation or treatment in the least restrictive environment. When the lower court reinstated its deinstitutionalization order, this time based on state law, the Supreme Court again remanded the case to the Third Circuit, ruling that under the principle of sovereign immunity, federal courts cannot order state officials to conform to state law.

This principle of sovereign immunity was applied in *Lelsz v. Kavanagh*, 807 F.2d 1243 (5th Cir. 1987), 11 MPDLR 97, also involving people with mental retardation. The Fifth Circuit ruled that a federal district court did not have jurisdiction to compel the state to establish community facilities, where the rights at issue were based on state, not federal, law. (Later developments in this case are discussed below.)

Post-Youngberg and Pennhurst II

Despite procedural difficulties, the lower court in *Pennhurst* did oversee a significant movement of institution residents into community living arrangements. While other court rulings support deinstitutionalization, the legal emphasis has shifted toward state court interpretations of state laws.

Federal courts still apply the U.S. constitution and federal laws in this context, but the idea of a right to treatment, habilitation, or other services in the least restrictive setting is not universal. At the same time, courts have been willing to go beyond a strict interpretation of *Youngberg, supra*, to find rights that approach, but do not fulfill, *Pennhurst*'s original mandate that all residents should be moved to smaller community arrangements.

Several federal appeals court decisions limit deinstitutionalization. The Eleventh Circuit found that minors who were voluntarily committed by their parents did not have a right to treatment in the least restrictive environment. *Doe v. Public Health Trust of Dade*

County, 696 F.2d 901 (11th Cir. 1983), 7 MDLR 220. The court suggested, however, that adults might have a constitutional right to such individualized treatment if it would help or cure their mental condition.

The Second Circuit was more absolute when, in *Society for Goodwill to Retarded Children, Inc. v. Cuomo*, 737 F.2d 1239 (2d Cir. 1984), 8 MPDLR 462, it overruled a lower court's deinstitutionalization decree. According to the appeals court, since there was no constitutional deprivation associated with being institutionalized *per se*, there could be no constitutional right to be in the community or in any other less restrictive setting.

In contrast, while the Third Circuit ruled against people with mental retardation who lived at home, the court recognized the importance of providing services to prevent the reinstitutionalization of people who lived in community residences. *Philadelphia Police & Fire Ass'n for Handicapped Children, Inc. v. City of Philadelphia*, 874 F.2d 156 (3d Cir. 1989) 13 MPDLR 235. The court found no equal protection violation in the City of Philadelphia's plan to cut services to people with mental retardation who lived at home, without making similar cuts for people with mental retardation who lived in community programs. The city found that people with mental retardation who lived in group homes were more likely to be reinstitutionalized if funding for them was cut, and stated that "[m]inimizing institutionalization clearly is a legitimate state interest." The court likewise found no substantive due process violation because the state had not affirmatively acted to restrain an individual's freedom to act on his own behalf which, according to the Supreme Court's analysis in *DeShaney v. Winnebago County Dep't of Social Servs.*, 489 U.S. 189 (1989), 13 MPDLR 104, was a prerequisite to the state's obligation to provide services. The state's prior provision of habilitation services was not determinative since, according to *DeShaney*, "'the State does not become the permanent guarantor of an individual's safety by having once offered him shelter.'"

In *Homeward Bound v. The Hissom Memorial Center*, No. 85-C-437-E (N.D. Okla. Jan. 12, 1990), 14 MPDLR 133, the court approved a consent decree that established a "framework for a community service system as an alternative to institutional care" for residents and former residents of a segregated institution. The court based its decision on federal due process, §504 of the Rehabilitation Act of 1973, and, for the first time, the Social Security Act regulations governing intermediate care facilities for persons with mental retardation (ICF/MR).

Similarly, the Fourth Circuit upheld a consent decree that ordered a number of services for an adult with mental retardation, including a detailed treatment plan, a case manager, suitable supportive services, and periodic evaluations. *Thomas S. v. Morrow*, 781 F.2d 367 (4th Cir. 1986), 10 MPDLR 101. The appeals court found that these less restrictive services were consistent with the principles articulated in *Youngberg*. Moreover, a federal district court found that the duty to exercise reasonable professional judgment articulated in *Youngberg* meant that the state had to ensure the provision of proper support services when professionals recommended that a resident be placed in the community. *Clark v. Cohen*, 613 F. Supp. 684 (E.D. Pa. 1985), 9 MPDLR 246.

Finally, even though the Fifth Circuit applied *Pennhurst II's* sovereign immunity limitations to discourage enforcement of state law claims against a Texas institution, (*see* discussion above), the lower court continued to move forward, ordering an investigation of one state school by an expert consultant; holding the state in contempt for failing to comply with a settlement agreement; and approving an implementation agreement that guaranteed funding for community-based residential placements, an independent advocacy system, and continued court monitoring for the next 10 years. *Lelsz v. Kavanagh*, 824 F.2d 372 (5th Cir. 1987), 11 MPDLR 325; 673 F. Supp. 828 (N.D. Tex. 1987), 11 MPDLR 400, *cert. denied*, 483 U.S. 1057 (1987). In 1991, the federal district court approved a final settlement agreement, requiring the closing of two state institutions and the creation of new "more intimate, community based programs." 783 F. Supp. 286 (N.D. Tex. 1991), 16 MPDLR 187.

Federal & State Statutes

In the late 1970s and early 1980s, plaintiffs had mixed success using federal statutes in their deinstitutionalization efforts. One federal court relied on several federal statutes, including the Developmental Disabilities Act, §1983, §504, and Pub. L. No. 94-142, to use individualized treatment plans to maximize the potential of each institution resident. *Garrity v. Gallen*, 522 F. Supp. 171 (D.N.H. 1981), 6 MDLR 9. The court stressed reasonable accommodation, refusing to construe §504 "so broadly as to require deinstitutionalization."

Kentucky ARC v. Conn, 674 F.2d 582 (6th Cir. 1982), 6 MDLR 167, *cert. denied*, 459 U.S. 1041 (1982), was an unsuccessful attempt to enjoin the construction of non-community-based facilities for people with developmental disabilities. As in *Garrity, supra*, the court held that §504 did not prohibit institutionalization, especially for certain people with severe and profound mental retardation for whom institutionalization might be the least restrictive alternative.

The Supreme Court's ruling in *Atascadero State Hosp. v. Scanlon*, 473 U.S. 234 (1985), 9 MPDLR 270, undermined reliance on federal statutes. Expanding upon *Pennhurst II*, a divided Court held that the principle of sovereign immunity limited the use of §504 and other federal statutes to states that unequivocally waive their immunity. Such a waiver must be based on express language, overwhelming textual implication, or unambiguous congressional intent.

With the declining reliance on federal statutes, state law has been an increasing source of relief. For example, the Wisconsin supreme court held that inadequate funding was an insufficient basis for a trial court's affirmance of the denial of community placements for people with developmental disabilities. *D.E.R. v. La Crosse County*, 449 N.W.2d 279 (Wis. Sup. Ct. 1990), 14 MPDLR 316. This state law trend has carried over to different types of institution-based litigation. *See, e.g., Rivers v. Katz*, and *Wisconsin ex rel. Jones v. Gerhardstein, supra*, at p. 46.

Decisionmaking Rights & Competency

Overview

The freedom to make decisions is fundamental to modern American concepts of liberty and autonomy. While at one time a person's status in a group often determined his or her rights and privileges, today, the right to self-determination generally is predominant.

Critics of coercive psychiatric and habilitative treatment have observed that, contrary to this general legal trend to move from group status to individual choice, laws and administrative actions are often still applied based on the status of citizens with various mental disabilities. In other words, laws that restrict or remove the freedom to choose from a person with a mental disability may unnecessarily reduce that person from someone who is able to act freely, to someone with the status of a "mentally disabled person" for whom family members, guardians, and/or the state will make choices.

In theory, an incompetency adjudication must precede the loss of decisionmaking rights, but the standards for making such determinations have changed over the years. Traditionally, being a person with a mental illness or mental retardation was sufficient for an incompetency finding. Moreover, a court's determination that someone met a state's civil commitment criteria was presumed to encompass incompetency, as well.

In the 1960s, the law began to reflect the fact that neither membership in a group nor being subject to involuntary civil commitment necessarily affected one's competency to make certain basic decisions. The trend was to focus on the individual's ability to care for his or her person or property. The current practice focuses more on whether the individual can make rational decisions, and views each type of decision separately. For someone who is found to be incompetent, the trend favors a determination based on what the individual would prefer if competent. As discussed below, states often require clear and convincing evidence of a person's intentions and, if this standard cannot be met, then courts may determine what course of action will be in the person's best interest.

Guardianship & Conservatorship

Guardianship often defines how an incompetency determination will be implemented. Potentially, it is the most inclusive form of substituted decisionmaking, in which a court gives a guardian the legal authority to make specified decisions for someone the court has found is unable to act for him or herself (the ward). Due to the significant loss of rights that typically follows a guardian's appointment, the procedures for appointing, monitoring, and removing guardians have come under increased scrutiny. In addition, more and more courts are limiting the guardian's powers to reflect the ward's particular needs, as determined in the incompetency proceeding.

Relatively recent studies have found that the statutory safeguards that exist to protect the ward's rights are not always implemented, or are implemented ineffectively. *See, e.g., Steps to Enhance Guardianship Monitoring* (1991), published by the ABA Commission on the Mentally Disabled and the Commission on Legal Problems of the Elderly, and the 1987 Associated Press report, "Guardians of the Elderly: An Ailing System." In 1988, the American Bar Association published 33 recommendations (31 of which were adopted by the ABA's House of Delegates), with commentary, on ways to improve the nation's guardianship system, including due process, incapacity determinations, court practices, guardian accountability, and the role of guardianship agencies. *See Guardianship: An Agenda for Reform.*

Traditionally, guardianships were divided into appointments that affected personal interests, known as guardianships of the person, and those that affected finances and property interests, known as guardianships of the estate or conservatorships. The most restrictive form, plenary guardianship, encompasses both personal and property rights. This basic division still exists, but the more modern view is reflected in "limited" guardianships, in which the court tailors the scope of the guardian's powers to the ward's individualized needs.

Moreover, even if a court establishes a plenary guardianship, some decisions remain beyond the guardian's authority, or the guardian will have to seek specific court authorization to make certain decisions. For example, guardians in most states cannot civilly commit a ward and, even where they can, courts have required more rigorous procedures than are usually required to implement a guardian's decision. New York's highest court held, in *In re Grinker*, 573 N.E.2d 536 (N.Y. Ct. App. 1991), 15 MPDLR

374, that courts cannot authorize the conservator of a person's estate to place the ward in a nursing home. Increased scrutiny is also applied when a guardian seeks to make decisions concerning intrusive medical procedures or a ward's sexual or reproductive rights. *See* discussion below.

Regardless of the nature of the guardianship proceeding, a due process hearing and a panoply of other safeguards are minimally required, including notice to the proposed ward and the right to attend the hearing. The threshold determination is whether the proposed ward is legally incompetent, a concept which is defined somewhat differently depending on the jurisdiction. The two leading formulations generally focus on either the ability to care for oneself or one's property, a functionally oriented approach, or the ability to make rational decisions, a definition oriented toward mental capacity.

Guardians can make substitute decisions for incompetent persons in a variety of situations. In recent years, the most controversial area has been medical treatment decisions. The right to refuse medication in institutions was discussed earlier, at pp. 29, 44-46. More recently, however, the issue of forcibly medicating individuals in the community has caused increased concern. As discussed in the Outpatient Commitment section, the threat of institutionalization is used to compel patients to take their medication in the community. *See* pp. 24,25.

Fundamental Decisionmaking Rights

In the past, decisions involving fundamental aspects of one's life were automatically taken away from individuals who were labelled mentally disabled or mentally ill. These decisions included: sterilization; the termination of parental rights; the choice of where to live; the termination of life-support systems; voting; marriage and divorce; disposing of one's property; diagnostic medical procedures; and selecting an attorney and other contract rights. Today, the more personal or intrusive the decision, the harder it is, legally, to restrict a person's decisionmaking rights. Indeed, the courts look far more closely at the individual's wishes or, if the person has not expressed or cannot express his or her wishes, attempt to determine what he or she would want if competent. And, as mentioned above, some decisions require court authorization and can never be made by a guardian on behalf of a ward.

As discussed earlier, advocates should understand the difference between competency and involuntary civil commitment. A client's commitment to an institution does not necessarily imply a lack of competence to make decisions, unless the commitment proceeding specifically addressed other competency issues. Moreover, different types of decisions require different degrees and kinds of competence, which often are reflected in different legal thresholds for determining competency.

Sexual Rights (Sterilization, Abortion)

All too often, people with mental disabilities have been sterilized unnecessarily, frequently without their consent. Despite periodic publicity, abuses continue, although they tend to occur on an individual basis, rather than en masse, as previously was the case. Three state supreme court cases reflect the circumstances in which a sterilization decision can be made without informed consent.

In *In re Hayes,* 608 P.2d 635 (Wash. Sup. Ct. 1980), 4 MDLR 154, the Washington supreme court established detailed guidelines to determine the existence of "the rare and unusual case [in which] sterilization is in the best interest of the retarded person." A trial court must find by clear, cogent and convincing evidence that the individual cannot make an informed decision about sterilization and is unlikely to be able to do so in the foreseeable future. The court also must find a need for contraception and that no reasonable alternative exists.

Maine's highest court held that a doctor was not entitled to summary judgment in a case charging him with the wrongful sterilization of a patient with mental retardation. *Chasse v. Mazerolle,* 580 A.2d 155 (Me. Sup. Jud. Ct. 1990), 15 MPDLR 57. The doctor did not comply with the statutory requirement that he consult both a physician and a surgeon to determine whether the person was competent to give consent and that the procedure was needed for genetic or therapeutic reasons. While the patient was incompetent to consent, there was no basis for concluding that the other doctors would have found that sterilization was necessary. *See In re Romero,* 790 P.2d 819 (Colo. Sup. Ct. 1990), 14 MPDLR 405.

In *McKinney v. McKinney*, 805 S.W.2d 66 (Ark. Sup. Ct. 1991), 15 MPDLR 374, the Arkansas supreme court struck down that part of the state's law that allows the involuntary sterilization of people with mental disabilities through "'direct medical channels'" with no judicial oversight and no right to notice, counsel, or a hearing.

In *In re Guardianship of K.M.*, 816 P.2d 71 (Wash. Ct. App. 1991), 16 MPDLR 47, the failure to appoint an independent counsel for an incompetent 15-year-old girl led to the reversal of a court order allowing her parents to consent to her sterilization.

A Massachusetts court reversed a decision that had held that a mother did not have the authority to consent to an abortion for her adult daughter with mental retardation. *In re Moe*, 579 N.E.2d 682 (Mass. App. Ct. 1991), 16 MPDLR 47. While the mother was the legal guardian, the trial court had made inadequate findings as to the ward's competency. Also, even if the ward was incompetent, the court gave inadequate consideration to her preference for an abortion. *See also In re Moe*, 432 N.E.2d 712 (Mass. Sup. Jud. Ct. 1982), 6 MDLR 143; *D.R. v. Daughters of Miriam Center for the Aged*, 589 A.2d 668 (N.J. Super. Ct. Ch. Div. 1990), 15 MPDLR 374; and *In re Jane Doe*, 533 A.2d 523 (R.I. Sup. Ct. 1987), 12 MPDLR 40.

Parental Rights

Mental illness, mental retardation, or substance abuse may be the basis for terminating someone's parental rights. As with other child custody issues, the overriding concern is the child's best interests. The mere existence of a mental disability is an insufficient basis for termination. Rather, the parent's condition must make him or her unable to care for the child; there must be, at least, a potential for harm (although courts need not wait for actual harm, *see Nebraska v. B.P.*, 432 N.W.2d 826 (Neb. Sup. Ct. 1988), 13 MPDLR 227); and, in many jurisdictions, even with supportive services (e.g., parenting classes) and/or treatment, the situation must be likely to persist for the foreseeable future. *See, e.g., West Virginia Dep't of Human Servs. v. Peggy F.*, 399 S.E.2d 460 (W. Va. Sup. Ct. 1990), 15 MPDLR 258.

Because terminating parental rights is an extreme and final measure, the U.S. Supreme court stated that due process requires clear and convincing evidence before the state can irrevocably sever a parent's rights to his or her child. *Santosky v. Kramer*, 455 U.S. 745 (1982), 6 MDLR 144. *See also In re R.A.D.*, 753 P.2d 862 (Mont. Sup. Ct. 1988), 12 MPDLR 430 (requiring determination of whether mother's rights were adequately protected without appointment of guardian ad litem), and *In re D.R.*, 541 A.2d 1260 (D.C. Ct. App. 1988), 12 MPDLR 430 (representation by an attorney required prior to relinquishment of parental rights).

In general, the state also has to prove that there are no viable alternatives to termination, *see Ex parte Ogle*, 516 So. 2d 243 (Ala. Sup. Ct. 1987), 12 MPDLR 260, and, where the state has established a rehabilitation plan, that the parent has willfully failed to comply with a material provision, i.e., one that would tend to correct or eliminate the underlying problem. *In re J.S.*, 417 N.W.2d 147 (Neb. Sup. Ct. 1987), 12 MPDLR 260.

Property & Other Rights

Mental capacity is an important factor in determining a person's ability to execute a valid will or contract (including a marriage contract), and to gain access to the courts. As stated in the guardianship section, the level of competency to carry out various functions differs, and incapacity to perform one or more of these activities does not, in and of itself, implicate the ability to perform the others. In fact, the level of capacity necessary to make a valid will or a contract is fairly low, and neither a mental illness nor mental retardation alone will suffice to prove incapacity. Nor will involuntary civil commitment or a declaration of incompetency for guardianship purposes necessarily establish the individual's incapacity with respect to other activities.

Testamentary capacity, i.e., the capacity to write a valid will, is measured according to whether people have a general understanding of the nature and extent of their property, the nature of what they are doing (signing a legally binding document) and its effect, the identities of the "natural objects of their bounty" (those, who by family or other relationship, would be expected to be beneficiaries), and an intention to distribute their property in the way they have stated in the will. *See, e.g., In re Estate of Raney*, 799 P.2d 986 (Mont. Sup. Ct. 1990), 15 MPDLR 148; *Cleveland v. Central Bank of the South*, 574 So. 2d 741 (Ala. Sup. Ct. 1990), 15 MPDLR 370; and *In re Estate of Loomis*, 810 P.2d 126 (Wyo. Sup. Ct. 1991), 15 MPDLR 479.

The *capacity to marry* requires the ability to understand the nature, duties, effects, and obligations of marriage. *See, e.g., Pape v. Byrd*, 582 N.E.2d 164 (Ill. Sup. Ct. 1991), 16 MPDLR 165; and *In re Estate of Hendrickson*, 805 P.2d 20 (Kan. Sup. Ct. 1991), 15 MPDLR 255.

Contractual capacity generally requires the abilities to understand the nature and consequences of the particular transaction, to act reasonably with respect to the transaction, and to agree to its terms. A party's incapacity may render a contract void, or only voidable, and the incapacitated party may have to prove that the other party knew of his or her condition. *See, e.g., Shoals Ford, Inc. v. Clardy*, 588 So. 2d 879 (Ala. Sup. Ct. 1991), 16 MPDLR 164; *Gilliland v. Carpenter*, 395 S.E.2d 779 (W. Va. Sup. Ct. 1990), 15 MPDLR 55; *Moser v. DeSetta*, 589 A.2d 679 (Pa. Sup. Ct. 1991), 15 MPDLR 370; and *Moore v. Brown*, 579 So. 2d 611 (Ala. Sup. Ct. 1991), 15 MPDLR 480.

Court access is an issue because mental disability may impair a person's ability to recognize that he or she has been harmed, can seek legal redress, and must take certain steps to seek relief. A key question often is whether the person's disability is sufficient to stop the statute of limitations from running. *See, e.g., O'Neal v. Division of Family Servs.*, 821 P.2d 1139 (Utah Sup. Ct. 1991), 16 MPDLR 288; *Lovelace v. Keohane*, No. 74,848 (Okla. Sup. Ct. Feb. 11, 1992), 16 MPDLR 288; *Canales v. Sullivan*, 936 F.2d 755 (2d Cir. 1991), 15 MPDLR 478; and *Barton-Malow Co., Inc. v. Wilburn*, 556 N.E.2d 324 (Ind. Sup. Ct. 1990), 14 MPDLR 533.

Health Care Decisions

Decisions may have to be made regarding whether various forms of medical treatment should be provided to or withdrawn from people who are incompetent to make these decisions for themselves. Some of these issues have been covered already for people who have been committed, civilly or criminally.

A substitute or surrogate decisionmaker may be appointed to make treatment decisions for people who no longer are (or never were) competent to make decisions on their own. The standard used in making decisions on behalf of incompetent people largely depends on whether the person, while competent, gave any indication of his or her wishes or preferences. Courts generally recognize such preferences, but if the person never indicated his or her wishes, or was never competent to do so, the court will apply either a version of the traditional "best interests" standard or the "substituted judgment" standard.

The best interests test is purportedly an objective standard which seeks to approximate what most reasonable, competent people in the particular community would do in the same situation. The substituted judgment test is a more subjective approach which attempts to determine what this particular patient would choose if he or she could make the decision. A newer standard combines the two, using substituted judgment when the person previously expressed his or her wishes or these wishes are ascertainable by clear and convincing evidence, but otherwise using the best interests test. *See* Parry, "A Unified Theory of Substitute Consent," 11 MPDLR 378.

Electroconvulsive Therapy

With a few exceptions, the modern law governing electroconvulsive therapy (ECT) is clear on four points. First, before ECT may be administered in most states, the patient must give voluntary, knowing, and competent consent, if he or she is capable of doing so. Second, ECT cannot be absolutely prohibited by statute or regulation. Third, in the absence of an incompetency adjudication or an emergency, most courts that have reviewed the matter have held that patients have an absolute right to accept or decline ECT. Fourth, if the patient has been adjudicated incompetent, a substitute decisionmaker generally must be appointed to exercise the patient's right to accept or decline ECT. *See* Parry, "Legal Parameters of Informed Consent Applied to Electroconvulsive Therapy," 9 MPDLR 162.

Most state statutes regulate the use of ECT, either specifically mentioning the procedure or generally limiting psychiatric treatments. Courts also set restrictions on the administration of ECT, requiring: a due process hearing for incompetent patients or those who withheld consent, *Price v Sheppard,* 239 N.W.2d 905 (Minn.

Sup. Ct. 1976), 1 MDLR 120; clear and convincing evidence of incapacity to consent before honoring a substitute decision, even for someone already placed under conservatorship, *Lillian F. v. Superior Court of Cal.*, 206 Cal. Rptr. 603 (Cal. Ct. App. 1984), 9 MPDLR 25; clear and convincing evidence that the treatment was needed, *Colorado ex rel. M.K.M.*, 765 P.2d 1075 (Colo. Ct. App. 1988), 13 MPDLR 209; and the use of substituted judgment, based on the decisionmaker's determination of what the patient would want. *See In re Detention of Schuoler*, 723 P.2d 1103 (Wash. Sup. Ct. 1986), 11 MPDLR 24.

In what appears to be a case of first impression nationwide, a New York court honored an involuntary patient's declaration, written before she became incompetent, withdrawing her consent to further ECT treatment. *In re Rosa M.*, No. 95-965-89 (N.Y. Sup. Ct. Nov. 27, 1991), 16 MPDLR 46.

"Right to Die"

Whether individuals have the right to refuse life-sustaining care has been one of the most controversial health care issues. Since the 1970s, courts have established that competent adults have the right to refuse such medical care, commonly referred to as the "right to die." This right is not absolute, however, but must be balanced against the state's interests in preserving life, preventing suicide, protecting the integrity of the medical profession, and protecting the interests of third parties.

The right to die assumes even greater significance when the patient is incompetent to make the decision. Often, the patient's next of kin or legal guardian will make the decision or, if the person, while competent, had executed a durable power of attorney covering health care decisions or a living will, then his or her designated surrogate can make the decision. When the patient does not have family or a legally designated surrogate, the court will have to decide. A key question is whether courts must also review or guide the decisions made by the patient's next of kin or guardian.

The law generally will recognize the treatment choice a patient indicated prior to losing capacity. A living will is the instrument used most commonly to express an individual's preferences concerning the type of life-sustaining medical treatment he or she wants to receive or refuse under certain circumstances, if he or she is unable to make that decision when the situation arises. Living wills generally become operative only when the person has a terminal illness, and cover what are generally considered "artificial" life-sustaining treatments.

Courts may honor expressions of such wishes even when they are not stated in a formal document that satisfies the state's "natural death act," *see In re Eichner*, 420 N.E.2d 64 (N.Y. Ct. App. 1981), 5 MDLR 160. But, especially when considering someone's oral expressions, courts may require clear and convincing evidence of the person's wishes. In *In re O'Connor*, 531 N.E.2d 607 (N.Y. Ct. App. 1988), 13 MPDLR 29, for example, New York's highest court required evidence that the "patient held a firm and settled commitment to the termination of life supports under the circumstances like those presented."

In the landmark "Cruzan" case, the U.S. Supreme Court upheld the application of a heightened standard of proof. The Court stated that "[t]he principle that a competent person has a constitutionally protected liberty interest in refusing unwanted medical treatment may be inferred from our prior decisions." Moreover, an incompetent person has a right to refuse life-sustaining care, including nutrition and hydration. *Cruzan v. Director, Missouri Dep't of Health*, 497 U.S. 261 (1990), 14 MPDLR 321. This right is not absolute, however, and given the state's strong interest in protecting incompetent patients from potential abuse by surrogate decisionmakers, the state can place reasonable restrictions on the exercise of this right, including requiring clear and convincing evidence of the patient's wishes. The Court also held that states need not accept the substituted judgment of close family members, since "there is no automatic assurance that the view of close family members will necessarily be the same as the patient's would have been had she been confronted with the prospect of her situation while competent."

Florida's highest court held that without prior court approval, a substitute decisionmaker can exercise the right to refuse treatment, including the right not to receive artificial nutrition and hydration, for someone "who has become incompetent and who, while competent, expressed his or her wishes orally or in writing." When such an expression is challenged or if court review is otherwise necessary, a written expression creates a "rebuttable presumption that constitutes clear and convincing evidence of the patient's wishes," while an oral expression leaves the surrogate with the burden of proof. *In re Guardianship of Browning*, 568 So. 2d 4 (Fla. Sup. Ct. 1990), 14 MPDLR 502.

Nevada's supreme court affirmed, without direction from the state legislature, that a competent adult has the right to refuse or discontinue life-sustaining medical treatment. *McKay v. Bergstedt*, 801 P.2d 617 (Nev. Sup. Ct. 1990), 15 MPDLR 152. The procedures used to implement this right will change if the patient has a terminal condition.

Massachusetts' highest court revoked a substituted judgment order authorizing the forcible administration of antipsychotic drugs to a competent patient. Moreover, all substituted judgment orders must be reviewed periodically and include a termination date. *Guardianship of Weedon*, 565 N.E.2d 432 (Mass. Sup. Jud. Ct. 1991), 15 MPDLR 258.

In a case of first impression, a California appeals court held that a competent patient does not have the right to be cryogenically preserved in the hope that he can be brought back to life if a cure is found for his brain disease. *Donaldson v. Van de Camp*, 4 Cal. Rptr. 2d 59 (Cal. Ct. App. 1992), 16 MPDLR 168. There is a distinction between the cessation of artificial life support where death is inevitable, and suicide through the intentional infliction of self-harm. Even if a patient has a fundamental right to take his or her own life, the state need not implement that right in any way the patient chooses.

For an historical perspective on the development of the law leading up to *Cruzan*, and the various state formulations and applications of surrogate decisionmaking standards, see *Superintendent of Belchertown State School v. Saikewicz*, 370 N.E.2d 417 (Mass. Sup. Jud. Ct. 1977), 2 MDLR 374 (institution resident with profound mental retardation, if competent, would not want chemotherapy); *In re Storar*, 420 N.E.2d 64 (N.Y. Ct. App. 1981), 5 MDLR 160 (blood transfusions should be given to a terminally ill patient with profound mental retardation over his mother's objections); *In re Farrell*, 529

A.2d 404 (N.J. Sup. Ct. 1987), 11 MPDLR 245 (competent patient, with the support of her family and physician, had the right to decline medical intervention); *In re Peter,* 529 A.2d 419 (N.J. Sup. Ct. 1987), 11 MPDLR 245 (unconscious patient has a right to die based on her prior indication that she did not want to receive extraordinary care, and a durable power of attorney giving her agent the authority to act on her behalf); *In re Jobes,* 529 A.2d 434 (N.J. Sup. Ct. 1987), 11 MPDLR 245 (family of patient in irreversible, vegetative state could exercise the patient's right to die, even in the absence of the patient's clearly expressed intent); *Rasmussen v. Fleming,* 741 P.2d 674 (Ariz. Sup. Ct. 1987), 11 MPDLR 329 (absent clear and convincing evidence of the patient's intent, the court permitted a guardian to consent to do not resuscitate orders for the patient based on the patient's best interests.) *See also* "The Court's Role in Decisionmaking Involving Incompetent Refusals of Life-Sustaining Care and Psychiatric Medications," 14 MPDLR 468, and "Decisionmaking in Authorizing and Withholding Life Sustaining Medical Treatment: From Quinlan to Cruzan," 13 MPDLR 482.

Infants With Severe Disabilities

Nowhere is the dilemma of the right to die for persons who are incompetent more poignant and controversial than when the patient is a newborn with severe disabilities. In "Baby Jane Doe," a series of nationally publicized legal decisions, state and federal courts allowed parents to choose nontreatment for their child. A New York court of appeals not only found that nontreatment was medically appropriate, but also that it was a reasonable decision made by concerned and loving parents. The state's highest court affirmed on different grounds, recognizing a danger in allowing an uninvolved third party to bring a legal action against the parents regarding their parental rights. *Weber v. Stony Brook Hosp.,* 467 N.Y.S.2d 685 (N.Y. App. Div. 1983), 456 N.E.2d 1186 (N.Y. Ct. App. 1983), 8 MPDLR 23.

Custody of a Minor, 434 N.E.2d 601 (Mass. Sup. Jud. Ct. 1982), 6 MDLR 226, affirmed a lower court's ruling that, based on substituted judgment, heroic efforts should not be used to extend the life of an infant with a fatal heart disease who had been abandoned by his parents.

In 1985, regulations were issued implementing the Child Abuse Amendments of 1984, 42 U.S.C. §5101-03 (Supp. 1985); U.S. Dep't of Health & Human Services, Child Abuse and Neglect Prevention & Treatment Program, 50 Fed. Reg. 14,878 (Apr. 15, 1985), codified at 45 C.F.R. §1340.5(c)(1). Under these amendments, child protective services agencies in states that receive federal funds must work to prevent life-threatening medical neglect of infants with disabilities, including the development of programs and procedures for responding to reports of such neglect. The ABA developed model procedures to assist states in implementing these requirements. Nicholson, Horowitz & Parry, "Model Procedures for Child Protective Service Agencies Responding to Reports of Withholding Medically Indicated Treatment from Disabled Infants With Life-Threatening Conditions," 10 MPDLR 221 (1986).

Exclusionary Zoning

With deinstitutionalization as the impetus, many more citizens with mental disabilities have tried to move into community settings, such as group or foster homes. Unfortunately, other citizens have often resisted this movement, giving rise to what has become known as the "NIMBY," or not in my backyard, attitude. Exclusionary zoning laws and restrictive covenants comprise a large part of that resistance.

In *Village of Euclid v. Ambler Realty Co.*, 272 U.S. 365 (1926), the U.S. Supreme Court defined zoning as a legitimate exercise of a locality's police power, as long as the particular ordinance bears a rational relationship to a permissible state objective. Zoning ordinances have been used with only limited success to block people with mental disabilities from entering the community. When such attempts have failed, however, residents have sometimes resorted to restrictive covenants, political pressure, and even violence.

State Laws & Policies

The most powerful expression of support for group homes is state legislation that has preempted local zoning ordinances and minimized the effects of restrictive covenants. *See, e.g., Rhodes v.*

Palmetto Pathway Homes, Inc., 400 S.E.2d 484 (S.C. Sup. Ct. 1991), 15 MPDLR 384, and *City of Livonia v. Dep't of Social Servs.*, 333 N.W.2d 151 (Mich. Ct. App. 1983), 7 MDLR 322. Also, lawsuits that seek to bar group homes based on covenants that restrict land use to single family residences often fail because courts find that, despite the absence of a biological relationship, the homes and their residents function similarly to a typical family. *See, e.g., Maull v. Community Living for the Handicapped, Inc.*, 813 S.W.2d 90 (Mo. Ct. App. 1991), 15 MPDLR 584, and *Double D Manor, Inc. v. Evergreen Meadows Homeowners' Ass'n*, 773 P.2d 1046 (Colo. Sup. Ct. 1989), 13 MPDLR 458. In addition, courts have upheld state laws that permit small groups of unrelated people with disabilities to live together as family units in residential neighborhoods. *See, e.g., Residential Management Sys., Inc. v. Jefferson County Plan Comm'n*, 542 N.E.2d 227 (Ind. Ct. App. 1989), 14 MPDLR 50, and *Mongony v. Bevilacqua*, 432 A.2d 661 (R.I. Sup. Ct. 1981), 5 MDLR 430.

Clearly articulated state policies have also persuaded courts, *see, e.g., Village of Maywood v. Health, Inc.*, 433 N.E.2d 951 (Ill. App. Ct. 1982), 6 MDLR 257, and such policies have been inferred from the acceptance of federal funds that encourage deinstitutionalization. Where ambiguities exist as to the state's policies, courts are more likely to rule in favor of localities, particularly in the presence of other factors, such as evidence that a group home is being run more like a business than like a family residence. *Civitans Care, Inc. v. Board of Adjustment of the City of Huntsville*, 437 So. 2d 540 (Ala. Civ. App. 1983), 8 MPDLR 37. In addition, while restrictive covenants are generally disfavored, courts will uphold them when they are set out unambiguously and do not conflict with existing state law. *Adult Group Properties, Ltd. v. Imler*, 505 N.E.2d 459 (Ind. Ct. App. 1987), 11 MPDLR 268. Otherwise, courts tend to overturn these covenants as being against the public interest. *Permian Basin Centers for Mental Health & Mental Retardation v. Alsobrook*, 723 S.W.2d 774 (Tex. Ct. App. 1987), 11 MPDLR 39.

City of Cleburne v. Cleburne Living Center, Inc., 473 U.S. 432 (1985), 9 MPDLR 278, is the only U.S. Supreme Court decision that directly addresses exclusionary zoning laws applied to people with mental disabilities. A 6-3 majority held that people with mental retardation, and by analogy other mental disabilities, are not a quasi-suspect class entitled to heightened equal protection scrutiny of laws restricting their rights. Applying the traditional rational relationship test, however, the Court found that a city zoning ordinance had denied equal protection by requiring that a group home for persons with mental retardation obtain a special use permit. Common sense demonstrations of the state's actual intent to exclude citizens with mental retardation rebutted the presumption of reasonableness accorded government actions.

Federal Law

In 1988, Congress took a major step toward addressing housing discrimination by adding people with disabilities to the classes of people protected by the Fair Housing Act (FHA). The Fair Housing Amendments Act of 1988, 42 U.S.C. §3601 et seq. (1990), defines disability in the same way as the Rehabilitation Act before it and the subsequently enacted Americans with Disabilities Act. *See* p.69. All of these laws not only cover people with a condition that affects a major life activity, but also people who have a history of such a disability or are regarded by others as having such a disability. The FHA does not cover people who use controlled substances illegally, or those who create "a direct threat to the health or safety of other individuals or whose tenancy would result in substantial physical damage to the property of others." Relying on, among other sources, the Americans With Disabilities Act, the Fourth Circuit held that drug-free participants in a substance abuse treatment program are "handicapped individuals" under the Fair Housing Amendments Act. *United States v. Southern Management Corp.*, 955 F.2d 914 (4th Cir.1992), 16 MPDLR 189.

The housing amendments also allow group home and other community residence operators to challenge exclusionary zoning practices and, according to the House Judiciary Committee's report, prohibit state or local regulations, restrictive covenants, and other zoning practices that conflict with the FHA. In addition, Title III of the ADA, covering public accommodations, provides that any type of facility that the FHA specifically addresses, either by covering it or expressly exempting it from coverage, is not considered a commercial facility under Title III. Also, while Title III does not cover residential facilities, the FHA may nevertheless protect a facility resident.

An Ohio federal court held, in *Marbrunak, Inc. v. City of Stow, Ohio*, No. 5:90 CV 0925 (N.D. Ohio July 29, 1991), 15 MPDLR 584, that the city violated the FHA by imposing permit requirements and onerous safety restrictions on single family residences for people with developmental disabilities. In *United States v. Puerto Rico*, 764 F. Supp. 220 (D.P.R. 1991), 15 MPDLR 495, a federal court granted a preliminary injunction to allow the federal government to investigate whether a zoning agency had violated the FHA in refusing to license a nursing home for people with severe mental and physical disabilities.

The Eighth Circuit upheld state and local dispersal schemes mandating that at least one-quarter mile separate residential programs for people with mental disabilities. *Familystyle of St. Paul, Inc. v. City of St. Paul*, 923 F.2d 91 (8th Cir. 1991), 15 MPDLR 164. The schemes did not violate the FHA or deny equal protection, and were consistent with the federal goal of guaranteeing "that residential treatment facilities will, in fact, be 'in the community,' rather than in neighborhoods completely made up of group homes that create an institutional environment."

Employment

Job applicants/employees with mental disabilities often are discriminated against in hiring, promotion, and retention because of stereotypes, misconceptions, or prejudice. Both the Rehabilitation Act of 1973 and the Americans With Disabilities Act (ADA) prohibit employment discrimination.

Rehabilitation Act

The Rehabilitation Act prohibits federal government agencies and organizations that receive federal funds or federal contracts in excess of certain dollar amounts from discriminating against qualified individuals with disabilities.

Section 501 mandates that each federal agency establish and

implement affirmative action programs that will provide "adequate hiring, placement, and advancement opportunities for" individuals with disabilities. 29 U.S.C. §791(b). This encompasses both nondiscrimination and affirmative action.

Similarly, §503 requires that any contractor with a federal contract in excess of $2,500 "shall take affirmative action to employ and advance in employment qualified handicapped individuals." 29 U.S.C. §793. Like §501, this encompasses both nondiscrimination and affirmative action. Any individual with a disability who believes that §503 has been violated can file an administrative complaint with the U.S. Department of Labor, Office of Federal Contract Compliance Programs, which is authorized to investigate and take appropriate action.

Section 504 covers not only employment, but all federally funded activities. It commands that "otherwise qualified" individuals with disabilities cannot "be excluded from participation in, be denied the benefits of, or be subjected to discrimination under any program or activity receiving Federal financial assistance or under any program or activity conducted by any Executive agency" or the postal service. 29 U.S.C. §794.

Americans With Disabilities Act

Title I of the ADA provides that, effective July 26, 1992, all employers with 25 or more employees (July 26, 1994 for employers with 15-24 employees) may not discriminate against an individual with a disability who is otherwise qualified for the job.

The term "discrimination" includes limiting, segregating, or classifying a job applicant or employee in a way that adversely affects the person's opportunities because of a disability; utilizing standards, criteria, or methods of administration that have the effect of discriminating on the basis of a disability; and not making reasonable accommodations to the known physical or mental limitations of an otherwise qualified individual with a disability, unless the employer can demonstrate that the accommodation would impose an undue hardship on the operation of the business. 42 U.S.C. §12112. *See* "Employment under the ADA: A National Perspective," 15 MPDLR 525.

The Equal Employment Opportunity Commission (EEOC) has

issued regulations implementing Title I. 29 C.F.R. Part 1630. *See* "Commentary," 15 MPDLR 13, and "Legislative and Regulatory Developments," 15 MPDLR 415, 522. The U.S. Department of Justice has also written regulations implementing Title II, which address employment discrimination by state and local governments. 28 C.F.R. Part 35.

Under the ADA, individuals with disabilities are afforded the same procedural and substantive protections that the Civil Rights Act provides to minorities and women. Because courts have held that §503 of the Rehabilitation Act does not create a private right of action, there has been very little litigation against employers not receiving federal financial assistance. Perhaps the most promising aspect of the ADA is the availability of litigation as a tool to eliminate employment discrimination in the private sector.

Definitions

Disability

Both the Rehabilitation Act and the ADA define an individual with a disability as any person who has a physical or mental impairment that substantially limits one or more of that person's major life activities. The definition also includes a person who has a record of having such an impairment, and one who is regarded as having such an impairment. *See* 29 U.S.C. §708(8), and 42 U.S.C. §12102(2). The EEOC's regulations further define mental impairment to include any mental or psychological disorder, such as mental retardation, organic brain syndrome, emotional or mental illness, and specific learning disabilities. 29 C.F.R. §1630.2(h)(2).

According to *School Bd. of Nassau County, Fla. v. Arline*, 480 U.S. 273 (1987), 11 MPDLR 110, the definition of a person with a disability is extremely broad, including a person who has an infectious disease such as tuberculosis. The definition thus covers many individuals with a mental disability. The definition specifically excludes transvestism, transsexualism, pedophilia, exhibitionism, voyeurism, gender identity disorders not resulting from a physical impairment, and other sexual behavior disorders; compulsive gambling, kleptomania, and pyromania; and psychoactive substance use disorders resulting from the current illegal use of drugs.

Qualified Individual with a Disability

Whether the Rehabilitation Act or the ADA will protect an individual with a disability depends on whether he or she is "qualified" to perform the specified job functions. While §504 does not contain a definition of "otherwise qualified," the ADA's language parallels §504 regulations in defining the term as "an individual with a disability who, with or without reasonable accommodation, can perform the essential functions of the employment position that such individual holds or desires." 42 U.S.C. §12111. The ADA further provides that consideration shall be given to the employer's judgment as to what job functions are essential, and if an employer has prepared a written description before advertising or interviewing applicants, this description will be considered evidence of essential functions.

The ADA provides that the terms disability and qualified individual with a disability do not include individuals currently engaging in the illegal use of drugs, but do include a person who successfully completed a supervised drug rehabilitation program and is no longer using drugs illegally, or has otherwise been successfully rehabilitated.

Reasonable Accommodation

While §504 itself does not define "reasonable accommodation," the ADA builds upon the §504 regulations in defining the term to include job restructuring; part-time or modified work schedules; reassignment to a vacant position; acquisition or modification of equipment or devices; appropriate adjustments to or modifications of examinations, training materials or policies; and the provision of qualified readers or interpreters. 42 U.S.C. §12111(9).

According to *Southeastern Community College v. Davis*, 442 U.S. 397, 413 (1979), 3 MDLR 240, §504 does not require an employer to "lower or effect substantial modifications of standards to accommodate a handicapped person." The Court ruled that a hearing-impaired applicant to a nursing school was not a "qualified handicapped person" because her hearing impairment would prevent her from participating in the program's clinical training. The Court found that if the program was modified by exempting the applicant from the clinical training requirements, "she would not receive even a rough equivalent of the training a nursing program normally gives." 442 U.S. at 410. The Court also found that the "purpose of [the] program was to train persons who could serve the nursing profession in all customary ways," and that the applicant would be unable, because of her hearing impairment, to perform some functions expected of a registered nurse. *Id.* Thus, the Court concluded that §504 did not require the school to make modifications that would result in "a fundamental alteration of the nature of the program." *Id.*

Moreover, under both §504 and the ADA, an employer need not make an accommodation that would impose an "undue hardship." The ADA defines the term as "an action requiring significant difficulty or expense" when considered in light of factors such as: the nature and cost of the accommodation; the overall financial resources of the facility involved in providing the accommodation, including the number of people employed at the facility and the effect on expenses, resources, and other aspects of the facility's operation; and the covered entity's overall financial resources, including the business' overall size, with respect to the number of its employees and the type, number, and location of its facilities. Whether an accommodation is "reasonable" will depend on the facts of the particular case.

Litigation

Private Right of Action

The U.S. Supreme Court's decision in *Consolidated Rail Corp. v. Darrone*, 465 U.S. 624 (1984), 8 MPDLR 113, established that individuals with disabilities have standing to pursue private actions for non-monetary relief under §504, and to recover back pay for intentional discrimination. Moreover, employees with disabilities who bring employment discrimination actions do not have to demonstrate that a primary purpose of the federal funds received by their employers is to provide employment. A 1988 amendment to the Rehabilitation Act, the Civil Rights Restoration Act, redefined "program or activity" to include institution-wide coverage. *See* 12 MPDLR 199. Thus, an entire institution is at risk if it discriminates on the basis of a disability, race, sex, or age, even when only a single unit within the institution receives federal funds.

A majority of courts have held that no private remedy is available under §503 because the section should be enforced exclusively by administrative means. *See, e.g., Rogers v. Frito Lay, Inc.*, 611 F.2d 1074 (5th Cir. 1980), *cert. denied*, 449 U.S. 889 (1980), 4 MDLR 83, 407. *See also* "Summary and Analysis," 4 MDLR 71.

There is no question that federal government applicants and employees have a private right of action under §501 of the Rehabilitation Act, by resorting to the rights, remedies, and procedures available under Title VII of the Civil Rights Act of 1964. Similarly, the ADA provides a private right of action following exhaustion of administrative remedies. *See* 42 U.S.C. §12117(a) and 29 U.S.C. §794a.

Section 504

In *Southeastern Community College v. Davis*, 442 U.S. 397 (1979), 3 MDLR 240, the U.S. Supreme Court found that an otherwise qualified person was "one who is able to meet all of a program's requirements in spite of his handicap." The Court stated that §504 required only that an "otherwise qualified" person not be excluded from participation "solely by reason of his handicap." This decision did not forbid recipients of federal monies from imposing reasonable qualifications for applicants. An employer or program administrator could not assume, however, that a person with a disability was unable to handle a particular job function.

Moreover, even if a person with a disability is unable to perform a certain task, the individual may not be denied employment or program access where reasonable accommodations can be made that will assist the individual and will not impose "undue financial and administrative burdens" on the employer or program. The U.S. Supreme Court affirmed this holding in *Arline, see* p. 69. *See also Nelson v. Thornburgh*, 567 F. Supp. 369 (E.D. Pa. 1983), 7 MDLR 469, *aff'd mem.*, 732 F.2d 146 (3d Cir. 1984), *cert. denied*, 469 U.S. 1188 (1985) (must provide readers, electronic devices, or other suitable accommodations to blind income maintenance workers), and *Strathie v. Dep't of Transp.*, 716 F.2d 227 (3d Cir. 1983), 7 MDLR 469 (person who wore hearing aid qualified to drive school bus).

A unanimous U.S. Supreme Court also ruled that a plaintiff need not show purposeful discrimination under §504. Rather, a showing of disparate-impact establishes a *prima facie* case. The Court emphasized that a recipient of federal funds must provide a qualified individual with a disability with "meaningful access" to a program benefit, even if doing so meant that the recipient had to make reasonable accommodations. *Alexander v. Choate,* 469 U.S. 287 (1985), 9 MPDLR 57.

In *Arline,* the U.S. Supreme Court also held that tuberculosis, and by analogy other contagious diseases such as AIDS, may be disabling conditions under §504. In determining whether an individual with a disability is "otherwise qualified" to be employed or to participate in a program, "an individualized inquiry" must be made that balances the individual's right to participate against the "legitimate concerns of . . . avoiding exposing others to significant health or safety risks." Courts must base their findings on reasonable medical judgments that assess the nature, duration, and severity of the risk to the individual and others, the probability the disease will be transmitted and will cause harm, and whether any "reasonable accommodation" can be made that will ameliorate unacceptable risks.

In an narrowly focused opinion, the U.S. Supreme Court held that a Veterans Administration regulation that viewed all cases of primary alcoholism as "willful misconduct" was not inconsistent with §504. The Court upheld the VA's irrebuttable presumption that alcoholism, without mental illness, was not a protected disability. *Traynor v. Turnage,* 485 U.S. 535 (1988), 12 MPDLR 297.

Applying U.S. Supreme Court decisions, the Second Circuit held that an applicant whose personality traits made him unsuitable to be a police officer was not an individual with a disability under §504. *Daley v. Koch,* 892 F.2d 212 (2d Cir. 1989), 14 MPDLR 149. The applicant was not diagnosed with a psychological illness or disorder, but was found unsuitable based on psychological interviews which determined, after he explained his four different jobs and four periods of unemployment in the three years prior to his application, that he used poor judgment, acted irresponsibly, and had poor impulse control.

In general, lower courts have held that police and transit officers who tested positive for drugs were not qualified individuals with disabilities under §504. *See, e.g., Copeland v. Philadelphia Police Dep't,* 840 F.2d 1139 (3d Cir. 1988), 12 MPDLR 356, and *Burka v. New York City Transit Auth.,* 680 F. Supp. 590 (S.D.N.Y. 1988), 12 MPDLR 356.

Finally, the Fourth Circuit recently reinstated a lawsuit by a teacher with a learning disability who could not pass the National Teachers Examination (NTE), a requirement for a teaching certificate. *Pandazides v. Virginia Bd. of Educ.,* 946 F.2d 345 (4th Cir. 1991), 15 MPDLR 579. A lower federal court had rejected the teacher's request to reasonably accommodate her disability by either waiving the exam, providing an oral exam, or giving her unlimited time to complete the exam. The appeals court found that factual questions existed as to whether the teacher was otherwise qualified despite her inability to pass the NTE, whether the NTE requirements represented the "essential functions" for a teacher position, and whether a test waiver was a reasonable accommodation.

Section 501

Federal courts examining §501 cases against the federal government have often utilized §504 case law and, because the definition of the terms individual with a disability, otherwise qualified individual with a disability, and reasonable accommodation are almost identical, these §501 cases also define rights under §504.

Plaintiffs with mental disabilities are not protected under §501 if their disability interferes with legitimate job requirements, they fight on the job, or they engage in criminal conduct. *Franklin v. U.S. Postal Serv.,* 687 F. Supp. 1214 (S.D. Ohio 1989), 12 MPDLR 362 (postal employee dismissed for engaging in violence on three occasions and refusing to take appropriate medication for her mental disability); *Fields v. Lyng,* 705 F. Supp. 1134 (D. Md. 1988), 13 MPDLR 361 (federal employee whose mental disability included anxiety about travel and a propensity to shoplift dismissed because he could not travel safely or be trusted); *Adams v. Alderson,* 723 F. Supp. 1531 (D.D.C. 1989), 14 MPDLR 149 (federal employee with a mental disability who was unable to refrain from violence against his supervisor was not qualified); *Pesterfield v. Tennessee Valley*

Auth., 941 F.2d 437 (6th Cir. 1991), 15 MPDLR 579 (federal employee's mental condition which made him unable to tolerate any criticism was not otherwise qualified); *Guice-Mills v. Derwinski*, 722 F. Supp. 188 (S.D.N.Y. 1991), 16 MPDLR 50 (Veterans Administration nurse who received treatment for stress was not qualified because she could not start work earlier than 10:00 a.m. and an accommodation would have imposed an undue burden on the VA hospital).

Many §501 cases hold that reassignment to a vacant position is not a reasonable accommodation, because a qualified individual with a disability is one "who with or without reasonable accommodation can perform the essential functions of the *position in question.*" *Carter v. Tisch*, 822 F.2d 465 (4th Cir. 1987), 11 MPDLR 411; and *Shea v. Tisch*, 870 F.2d 786 (1st Cir. 1989), 13 MPDLR 231. See 29 C.F.R. §1613.702(f). One of the major differences between the Rehabilitation Act and the ADA is that the ADA states that reassignment is an example of a reasonable accommodation. 42 U.S.C. §12111(9).

Alcoholism generally is a disability for purposes of the Rehabilitation Act, and many of the cases were filed under §501. *See Whitlock v. Donovan*, 598 F. Supp. 126 (D.D.C. 1984), 9 MPDLR 34, *aff'd without opinion*, 790 F.2d 964 (D.C. Cir. 1986). Courts differ as to what federal agencies must do to reasonably accommodate employees with alcoholism. *See Burchell v. Dep't of the Army*, 679 F. Supp. 1393 (D.S.C. 1988), 12 MPDLR 358; *Ferguson v. U. S. Dep't of Commerce*, 680 F. Supp. 1514 (M.D. Fla. 1988), 12 MPDLR 358; *Rodgers v. Lehman*, 869 F.2d 253 (4th Cir. 1989), 13 MPDLR 361. *Cf. Butler v. Thornburgh*, 900 F.2d 871 (5th Cir. 1990), 14 MPDLR 330; *Fuller v. Frank*, 916 F.2d 558 (9th Cir. 1990), 15 MPDLR 156.

Finally, under §501's affirmative action requirements, plaintiffs with mental disabilities have been successful in obtaining "excepted service" positions, in which people are hired outside the regular federal civil service guidelines with lesser benefits. Once excepted service employees begin performing the same work as regular employees, however, courts have found that they are entitled to similar benefits. *See Shirey v. Devine*, 670 F.2d 1188 (D.C. 1982),

6 MDLR 154, and *Allen v. Heckler,* 780 F.2d 64 (D.C. Cir. 1985), 10 MPDLR 111.

Education

Individuals with Disabilities Education Act

The Individuals with Disabilities Education Act (IDEA) (formerly known as the Education for All Handicapped Children Act or EAHCA), 20 U.S.C. §1400 et seq., and its implementing regulations, comprise a comprehensive scheme to ensure a free, appropriate, public education for all children with disabilities.

Amendments to the IDEA have expanded its scope to cover all children with disabling conditions from birth to age 21. 20 U.S.C. §§1471 to 1485. These conditions include mental illnesses, mental retardation and other developmental disabilities, learning disabilities, chronic health problems, physical impairments, hearing impairments and deafness, speech impairments, and visual impairments and blindness. The IDEA applies in all settings regardless of whether the child with a qualifying disability resides with his or her parents, in an institution, or in a group or foster home.

The IDEA entitles a child to a range of services, including early identification and assessment of disabilities, psychological services, medical services for diagnostic or evaluative purposes, special transportation to school and activities within school, and parent counseling. The child also may be entitled, at the school district's or state's expense, to attend special schools or to an education in a residential setting.

Further, the IDEA and its regulations mandate that special education services be provided consistent with the concept that, to the greatest extent possible, the child should be "mainstreamed" with children who do not have disabilities in order to minimize the stigma that frequently attaches to students who are placed in "special" education programs.

Finally, the IDEA requires that the school district periodically develop an Individualized Education Program (IEP) for every child found to be disabled. The IEP is the product of an evaluation conducted by the school district that assesses the child's abilities and educational needs, and determines what special education services are necessary. The IEP enumerates learning goals for the child and describes the services that the school district will be required to provide in order to meet those goals.

Section 504 & the ADA

The educational rights of a person with a disability may also be advanced under §504 of the Rehabilitation Act of 1973 and the ADA. Section 504 applies to any agency or organization that receives federal funds, including elementary, secondary, and post-secondary education programs, and prohibits discrimination against individuals with disabilities. *See* discussion p. 68. The applicable §504 regulations are found at 34 C.F.R. Part 104.

Section 504, the IDEA, and the ADA complement each other. Section 504 reinforces aspects of the IDEA, particularly that people with disabilities are entitled to a "free, appropriate public education," and that the educational program should be tailored to the individual's particular needs.

The ADA provides that state and local governments and public accommodations may not discriminate against qualified individuals with disabilities. Title II of the ADA applies to public nursery, elementary, secondary, undergraduate, and postgraduate schools, and to other places of education, while Title III applies to private schools and programs.

Free, Appropriate, Public Education

In *Board of Educ. of the Hendrick Hudson Central School Dist. v. Rowley*, 458 U.S. 176 (1982), 6 MDLR 235, the U.S. Supreme Court first defined what constitutes an appropriate education. Amy Rowley was a deaf elementary school student who needed a sign language interpreter to help maximize her educational potential. The Court determined that because Amy already was receiving special services that allowed her to outperform the average child in her class, she was not entitled to an interpreter. A free, appropriate, public education did not entitle her to the best possible education, only an education that guaranteed that she could benefit from her IEP.

Courts have subsequently expanded *Rowley* to require that a school district provide "meaningful educational benefits" rather than just "some benefit." *See, e.g., Polk v. Central Susquehanna Intermediate Unit 16*, 853 F.2d 171 (3d Cir. 1988), 12 MPDLR 448. Moreover, school districts must provide an appropriate education to children regardless of how they functioned in school. *See Abney ex rel. Kantor v. District of Columbia*, 849 F.2d 1491 (D.C. Cir. 1988), 12 MPDLR 530 (teenager functioning as a one-month old must be given an appropriate education); and *Timothy W. v. Rochester, N.H., School Dist.*, 875 F.2d 954 (1st Cir. 1989), 13 MPDLR 463 (must provide a special education to a child with multiple disabilities even if he could not benefit from that education).

Related Services

The IDEA defines "related services" as any of a wide range of supportive services such as transportation, speech pathology, audiology, physical therapy, and recreation. The term also covers certain medical and counseling services if they are used for diagnostic and evaluation purposes only, and are needed to enable a child to benefit from special education. 20 U.S.C. §1407(17).

In *Irving Indep. School Dist. v. Tatro*, 468 U.S. 883 (1984), 8 MPDLR 392, a unanimous U.S. Supreme Court held that a child with spina bifida was entitled to services to enable her to empty her bladder during the school day. The girl's IEP had to include this "related service," where the school nurse did not need a physician's assistance to carry out the procedure, and the procedure was needed to allow the student to benefit from her special education.

In general, the IDEA requires the provision of psychological services, unless they must be provided by a physician or do not relate directly to the student's education. *Max M. v. Thompson*, 592 F. Supp. 1437 (N.D. Ill. 1984), 8 MPDLR 547. Moreover, private residential placements may be covered if the student's mental disability, left untreated, would prevent him or her from benefiting from special education in a public setting. *Todd D. v. Andrews*, 933 F.2d 1576 (11th Cir. 1991), 15 MPDLR 500 (child's placement in an out-of-state psychiatric facility did not violate the IDEA requirement that the child be placed in the least restrictive environment).

Placement

While a number of cases discuss financial issues related to private placements, *see* discussion *infra,* parents also litigate whether their children should be placed in "mainstreamed" classes in the public school or in public school special education programs. In *Greer v. Rome City School Dist.,* 950 F.2d 688 (11th Cir. 1991), 16 MPDLR 203, the Eleventh Circuit held that the IDEA's mainstreaming requirement prohibited a school district from placing a child with Down syndrome in a special education program outside of her neighborhood. *Chris C. v. Gwinnett County School Dist.,* 780 F. Supp. 804 (N.D. Ga. 1991), 16 MPDLR 317, held that a student with Down syndrome should be placed in a public program for students with moderate rather than mild mental retardation. Finally, *Board of Educ., Sacramento City Unified School Dist. v. Holland,* 786 F. Supp. 874 (E.D. Cal. 1992), 16 MPDLR 316, ordered a school district to place a child with moderate mental retardation in a regular class rather than a special education program.

Financial Issues

Under certain circumstances, parents may be reimbursed for the expenses they incur in placing their child in a private special education program. In *School Comm. of the Town of Burlington v. Department of Educ. of Mass.,* 471 U.S. 359 (1985), 9 MPDLR 203, the U.S. Supreme Court ruled that parents may be entitled to reimbursement even if they unilaterally place their child in a private school. The critical factor is whether the parents ultimately prevail in the administrative and judicial proceedings. Conversely, school districts and state education agencies may recover private tuition payments they have made on a child's behalf if the courts ultimately decide that the proposed public school placement was appropriate.

Following *Burlington,* many courts have considered placement and tuition reimbursement issues for children with mental disabilities. *See, e.g., Jefferson County Bd. of Educ. v. Breen,* 853 F.2d 853 (11th Cir. 1988), 12 MPDLR 528 (out-of-state placement was appropriate for a child with severe psychiatric problems); *Drew v. Clarke County School Dist.*, 877 F.2d 927 (11th Cir. 1989), 13 MPDLR 532 (residential facility was appropriate for a child with autism and mental retardation); *Clovis Unified School Dist. v. California Office of Admin. Hearings*, 903 F.2d 635 (9th Cir. 1990), 14 MPDLR 339 (school district did not have to pay for child's treatment in a psychiatric hospital); *Doe v. Alabama Dep't of Educ.*, 915 F.2d 651 (11th Cir. 1990), 15 MPDLR 76 (non-residential program was appropriate for a student with mental illness); *Ash v. Lake Oswego School Dist. No. 7J*, 766 F. Supp. 852 (D. Or. 1991), 15 MPDLR 595 (child with autism entitled to private residential education); *G.D. v. Westmoreland School Dist.*, 930 F.2d 942 (1st Cir. 1991), 15 MPDLR 396 (parents denied reimbursement for a special day school and residential placement for a child with a learning disability); and *Andersen v. District of Columbia*, 877 F.2d 1018 (D.C. Cir. 1989), 13 MPDLR 534 (no private school for a child with a learning disability).

Compensatory Education & Extended School Year

Courts have awarded compensatory education beyond age 21 to children with mental disabilities who were denied their right to a free, appropriate education before they turned 21. *See, e.g., Burr ex rel. Burr v. Ambach*, 863 F.2d 1071 (2d Cir. 1989), 14 MPDLR 161; *Lester H. v. Gilhool*, 916 F.2d 865 (3d Cir. 1990), 15 MPDLR 174, *cert. denied, Chester Upland School Dist. v. Lester H.*, 111 S. Ct. 1317 (1991); *Mrs. C. v. Wheaton*, 916 F.2d 69 (2d Cir. 1990), 15 MPDLR 175; and *Valerie J. v. Derry Co-op School Dist.*, 771 F. Supp. 483 (D.N.H. 1991), 16 MPDLR 68.

Courts differ, however, on whether children are entitled to an extended school year to give them an appropriate education. *Compare Johnson v. Independent School Dist. No. 4 of Bixby, Tulsa County, Okla.*, 921 F.2d 1022 (10th Cir. 1990), 15 MPDLR 78 (student with profound autism, moderate mental retardation, and seizures entitled to summer school) *with Cordrey v. Euckert*, 917 F.2d 1460 (6th Cir. 1990), 15 MPDLR 174 (student with severe developmental delays and autistic like behavior not entitled to extended school year).

The Fifth Circuit recently held that a child with mental and physical disabilities was not entitled to a full seven-hour school day of programming. *Christopher M. v. Corpus Christi Indep. School Dist.*, 933 F.2d 1285 (5th Cir. 1991), 15 MPDLR 500. Instead, a four-hour school day was appropriate because the boy's disabilities limited his ability to receive educational benefits.

Expulsion of Students

The U.S. Supreme Court held, in *Burlington, supra*, that once an IEP is fixed through consensus or administrative or judicial proceedings, it is assumed to be correct unless both the school district and the parents change their minds. This is known as the "stay put" provision. 20 U.S.C. §1415(e)(3).

In *Honig v. Doe*, 484 U.S. 305 (1988), 12 MPDLR 172, the Supreme Court applied the "stay put" provision to prevent school officials from expelling students whose emotional disturbances caused their dangerous or disruptive behavior. While schools may impose a maximum 10-day suspension on students with disabilities who create an immediate danger to themselves or others, any further suspension must be implemented through an IEP.

Following *Honig*, a number of lower courts reviewed school district attempts to expel students with mental disabilities. *See, e.g., Christopher W. v. Portsmouth School Comm.*, 877 F.2d 1089 (1st Cir. 1989), 13 MPDLR 531 (suit by student with behavioral problems challenging disciplinary sanctions dismissed for failure to exhaust administrative remedies); *Hayes v. Unified School Dist. No. 377*, 877 F.2d 809 (10th Cir. 1989), 13 MPDLR 531 (failure to exhaust administrative remedies led to dismissal of parents' suit against school officials who had placed children with mental disabilities in time-out rooms following in-school suspensions); *Carey ex rel. Carey v. Maine School Admin. Dist. 17*, 754 F. Supp. 906 (D. Me. 1990), 15 MPDLR 279 (dismissal of parents' challenge to expulsion of their son, a child with an emotional disturbance, who brought a gun to school).

Immunity

In enacting the 1986 Rehabilitation Amendments, Congress

provided that: "A State shall not be immune under the Eleventh Amendment to the Constitution of the United States from suit in Federal Court for a violation of section 504 of the Rehabilitation Act of 1973." 42 U.S.C. §2000d-7(b). This amendment overruled *Atascadero State Hosp. v. Scanlon*, 473 U.S. 234 (1985), 9 MPDLR 270, in which the U.S. Supreme Court had held that states are entitled to eleventh amendment immunity from §504 suits for damages.

Congress also amended the IDEA in 1986. The Handicapped Children's Protection Act (HCPA) provides courts with discretion to award reasonable attorneys' fees to the parents or guardians of children with disabilities who have prevailed in IDEA lawsuits. 20 U.S.C. §1415(e). The HCPA requires the exhaustion of administrative remedies and, if an action is filed under the U.S. Constitution or §504, and the IDEA, the IDEA's administrative remedies must first be exhausted.

The U.S. Supreme Court held that Congress, in enacting the IDEA, did not waive the states' sovereign immunity. *Dellmuth v. Muth*, 491 U.S. 223 (1989), 13 MPDLR 377. A waiver of sovereign immunity must be both "unequivocal and textual." In 1990, however, Congress amended the IDEA, stating that: "A State shall not be immune under the eleventh amendment to the Constitution of the United States from suit in Federal court for a violation of this Act." 20 U.S.C. §1403(a). This covers violations that occurred in whole or in part after October 30, 1990. 20 U.S.C. §1403(c).

The ADA also contains a section waiving the state's eleventh amendment immunity. 42 U.S.C. §12202.

Damages

A unanimous U.S. Supreme Court recently ruled that a damage remedy is available for an action brought to enforce Title IX of the Education Amendments of 1972, 20 U.S.C. §§1681-1688. *Franklin v. Gwinnett County Public Schools*, 112 S. Ct. 1028 (1992). A high school student had filed a damages action in a federal district court, alleging continual harassment and abuse by a teacher. The Supreme Court stated the general rule that "absent clear direction to the contrary from the Congress, the federal courts have the power to award any appropriate relief in a cognizable cause of action brought pursuant to a federal statute."

The Court clearly recognized that a damage remedy would also be available under §504. To support its finding that Congress did not intend to limit remedies, the Court cited the Civil Rights Remedies Equalization Amendment of 1986, 42 U.S.C. §2000d-7, in which Congress abrogated the states' eleventh amendment immunity under Title IX, Title VI, and §504, and the Civil Rights Restoration Act of 1987, in which Congress broadened the coverage of these antidiscrimination provisions.

This decision follows a recent amendment to Title VII of the Civil Rights Act of 1964, which allows victims of intentional discrimination, including individuals with disabilities, to seek monetary damages, but places a cap on awards. *See* Civil Rights Act of 1991, S. 1745. "Legislative and Regulatory Developments," 15 MPDLR 613. Changes in the Civil Rights Act's enforcement provision are also important because the remedies available for employment discrimination under the ADA are linked directly to those available under Title VII.

Private Insurance

Coverage

A growing controversy in the 1990s concerns discrimination on the basis of mental disability by private insurers trying to reduce their claims' liability. Too often, insurance companies treat applicants with mental disabilities differently from other applicants, with little regard to the actual risk they represent. Thus, persons with mental disabilities often pay higher premiums, are ineligible for coverage, or are excluded from benefits when they file claims.

In 1987, the Supreme Court upheld a Massachusetts statute that required private insurance companies to provide mental health coverage as part of their general health care insurance plans. Two federal laws that regulate privately-delivered employee health insurance plans did not preempt the state statute. *Metropolitan Life Ins. Co. v. Massachusetts*, 471 U.S. 724 (1985), 9 MPDLR 282.

As of April 1992, 30 states and the District of Columbia required benefits for treatment of mental illness, but only 17 of them actually mandate inpatient and/or outpatient treatment, and the required level of benefits varies widely. *See* "State MH Mandates Outperform Federal Proposals," *Psychiatric News* (Apr. 17, 1992).

In determining to what extent insurance policies cover mental health care, courts often examine the policy's terms and definitions, and generally resolve ambiguities in favor of the insured. Courts also review any information an insurance applicant may have withheld from an insurance company, deciding whether the applicant made a material misrepresentation. This determination often focuses on whether the company would have extended coverage had it known this information.

The Eighth Circuit held that an affective mood disorder was subject to the coverage limitation for mental illness found in a policy regulated by the Employee Retirement Income Security Act (ERISA), 29 U.S.C. §1001 et seq. The trial court had erred in relying on "experts to define terms that were specifically written for and targeted toward laypersons." *Brewer v. Lincoln Nat'l Life Ins. Co.*, 921 F.2d 150 (8th Cir. 1990), 15 MPDLR 272. *See also Phillips v. Lincoln Nat'l Life Ins. Co.*, 774 F. Supp. 495 (N.D. Ill. 1991), 16 MPDLR 62 (" 'mental illness' " should be construed to include organic brain syndrome); and *Kunin v. Benefit Trust Life Ins. Co.*, 910 F.2d 534 (9th Cir. 1990), 14 MPDLR 516 (" 'mental illness' " should be construed to include autism).

A key issue in suicide and attempted suicide cases often involves policy exclusions for " 'intentional' " injuries. In *Reinking v. Philadelphia Am. Life Ins. Co.*, 910 F.2d 1210 (4th Cir. 1990), 15 MPDLR 72, the insurer had to pay both medical benefits and attorneys' fees because the insured was not competent to decide to commit suicide.

An insurer may try to deny life insurance benefits based on the insured's failure to disclose an unrelated mental disability. The Alaska supreme court held that an insured's failure to disclose a suicide attempt and alcoholism was admissible evidence, even though he died of a ruptured aorta. *Petersen v. Mutual Life Ins. Co. of N.Y.*, 803 P.2d 406 (Alaska Sup. Ct. 1990), 15 MPDLR 274.

Payment under a homeowner's policy may depend on the applicability of intentional harm exclusions. In *Shelter Mut. Ins. Co. v. Williams*, 804 P.2d 1374 (Kan. Sup. Ct. 1991), 15 MPDLR 275, the insurer did not have to pay benefits after the insured's insane son went on a shooting spree in his father's home. The son's intent to do harm was based on his understanding of the physical consequences of his acts, not his ability to tell right from wrong. *See also Germantown Ins. Co. v. Martin*, 595 A.2d 1172 (Pa. Super. Ct. 1991), 15 MPDLR 61 ("senseless, irrational and incomprehensible" acts were intentional).

In contrast, the Minnesota supreme court found no intent to harm where the insured did "not know the nature or wrongfulness of an act, or . . . is deprived of the ability to control his conduct regardless of any understanding of the nature of the act or its wrongfulness." *State Farm Fire & Casualty Co. v. Wicka,* 474 N.W.2d 324 (Minn. Sup. Ct. 1991), 16 MPDLR 61. *See also Nationwide Mut. Fire Ins. Co. v. May*, 860 F.2d 219 (6th Cir. 1988), 13 MPDLR 128 (homeowner's son who set fire could not understand physical consequences of his acts).

Reimbursement of Service Providers

A health insurance issue which spills over to government entitlement programs is which mental health professionals, in addition to medical doctors, will be reimbursed for their services. The answer often turns on whether the professionals are acting under the supervision of, or on orders from, a medical doctor.

In 1982, the U.S. Supreme Court held that a woman who was denied coverage under her employer's prepaid group health plan for the costs of a clinical psychologist's services had standing to sue for antitrust violations under §4 of the Clayton Act. *Blue Shield of Va. v. McCready*, 457 U.S. 465 (1982), 6 MDLR 225. The health plan reimbursed participants for the cost of a psychiatrist's care, but denied reimbursement for the psychologist's services because the costs were not billed through a physician. The suit alleged that Blue Shield had conspired with the Virginia Neuropsychiatric Society to exclude psychologists from receiving compensation under the plan.

An Oregon court held that state law allows a health maintenance organization (HMO) to limit reimbursement to services provided by psychologists who are affiliated with a specified organization. *Oregon Psychological Ass'n v. Physicians Ass'n of Clackamas County, Inc.*, 816 P.2d 686 (Or. Ct. App. 1991), 16 MPDLR 63.

Confidentiality

Prejudice and the stigma associated with mental disabilities underscore the need for confidentiality. Two legal concerns are particularly important: a therapist's duty to warn or otherwise protect third parties, and patient or third party access to a patient's records.

Duty to Protect

In the seminal case, *Tarasoff v. Board of Regents of the Univ. of Cal.,* 529 P.2d 553 (Cal. Sup. Ct. 1974), *aff'd on rehearing,* 551 P.2d 334 (Cal. Sup. Ct. 1976), 1 MDLR 128, the California supreme court held that when a "therapist determines, or pursuant to the standards of his profession should determine, that his patient represents a serious danger of violence to another, he incurs an obligation to use reasonable care to protect the intended victim." To fulfill this duty, the therapist may have to warn the victim or notify the police. The American Psychiatric Association expressed concern that breaching the confidential relationship would jeopardize the patient's trust and compromise therapy, but the court held that "the public policy favoring protection of the confidential character of patient-psychotherapist communications must yield to the extent to which disclosure is essential to avert danger to others."

Fears that a duty to protect would lead to significant incursions into patients' privacy have been realized, but overall the intrusions have been less widespread than was predicted. In "The Psychotherapist's Duty to Protect Third Parties from Harm," 11 MPDLR 141, a practicing psychiatrist concluded that even though the duty to protect subjects therapists to potential liability, liability is rarely imposed. The most significant consequence is the chilling effect that inconsistent application of the duty has on the psychiatric profession.

Some courts have expanded *Tarasoff,* imposing a duty to warn likely victims, even if they are unidentified, *Jablonski v. United States,* 712 F.2d 391 (9th Cir. 1983), 7 MDLR 401, or any reasonably foreseeable victim, *Lipari v. Sears Roebuck & Co.,* 497 F. Supp. 185 (D. Neb. 1980), 4 MDLR 313, and *Bradley Center v.*

Wessner, 296 S.E.2d 693 (Ga. Sup. Ct. 1982), 7 MDLR 123. *Hedlund v. Superior Court of Orange County,* 669 P.2d 41 (Cal. Sup. Ct. 1983), 8 MPDLR 50, held that "a negligent failure to diagnose dangerousness in a *Tarasoff* action is as much a basis for liability as is a negligent failure to warn a known victim once such diagnosis has been made."

The Wisconsin supreme court went so far as to find that therapists can be held liable for unforeseeable consequences to unforeseeable plaintiffs. The court held, in *Schuster v. Attenberg,* 424 N.W.2d 159 (Wis. Sup. Ct. 1988), 12 MPDLR 371, that a third party could state a cause of action for a psychotherapist's failures to warn a patient of the side effects of medication, to warn his family of his potential dangerousness, and to seek the patient's commitment.

While the *Tarasoff* duty normally extends only to identifiable victims, some courts have limited the duty even further, *Brady v. Hopper,* 751 F.2d 329 (10th Cir. 1984), 9 MPDLR 209, or refused to recognize a duty altogether, *Cole v. Taylor,* 301 N.W.2d 766 (Iowa Sup. Ct. 1981), 5 MDLR 261, and *Shaw v. Glickman,* 415 A.2d 625 (Md. Ct. Spec. App. 1980), 4 MDLR 313.

In *Currie v. United States,* 836 F.2d 209 (4th Cir. 1987), 12 MPDLR 17, the Fourth Circuit refused to impose liability against a psychiatrist who had not initiated involuntary commitment proceedings but had warned the victim, notified law enforcement officials, and repeatedly recommended voluntary commitment. A mere error in judgment was insufficient to impose liability, and the court focused on the "good faith, independence, and thoroughness" of the therapist's actions.

Therapist-Patient Privilege

States have enacted laws that confer privileged status on information revealed in a therapeutic setting, and generally require the patient's consent before such information can be revealed. These laws may apply to physicians generally, to psychiatrists or psychologists specifically, or more broadly, to psychotherapists, which may include social workers and other counselors. The privilege is not absolute, and generally pertains only to communications that were necessary for diagnosis or treatment. Moreover, statutes contain exceptions and courts may be called upon to decide whether other competing interests outweigh the patient's privacy interest and other treatment concerns. The most common exceptions apply to civil commitment proceedings, court-ordered exams, instances of suspected child abuse, and when a patient raises his or her mental condition in the course of a civil or criminal case (the latter constitutes a waiver, rather than an exception, and the contexts in which this may occur were discussed previously, *see* p. 28).

The Sixth Circuit recognized a limited therapist-patient privilege which did not preclude the enforcement of grand jury subpoenas issued to psychiatrists during an insurance fraud investigation. The information sought was limited to the patients' identities and dates and lengths of treatment. *In re Subpoena Served Upon Zuniga*, 714 F.2d 632 (6th Cir. 1983), 7 MDLR 451.

Arkansas v. Sypult, 800 S.W.2d 402 (Ark. Sup. Ct. 1990), 15 MPDLR 276, invalidated a state law which had created an exception to the physician/therapist-patient privileges in sex abuse cases. The statutory exception conflicted with court-created rules making a sex abuse defendant's statements to his physician/therapist inadmissible.

The Indiana supreme court held that a defendant should have been allowed to depose a murder victim's social worker and psychologist. There was no social worker-patient privilege, and the psychologist-patient privilege did not apply to disclosures related "directly to the fact or immediate circumstances" of a homicide. *Jorgensen v. Indiana*, 574 N.E.2d 915 (Ind. Sup. Ct. 1991), 15 MPDLR 589.

In *Vermont v. Curtis*, 597 A.2d 770 (Vt. Sup. Ct. 1991), 16 MPDLR 65, the state supreme court ruled that the state privilege statute for mental health professionals did not automatically cover a social worker investigating a sexual assault.

The Colorado supreme court held that the attorney-client privilege protects a criminal defendant's statements to a defense psychiatrist, even after the defendant raises an impaired mental condition defense. *Miller v. District Court*, 737 P.2d 834 (Colo. Sup. Ct. 1987), 11 MPDLR 263. The California supreme court held, however, that a capital murder defendant's statements to his psychotherapist about his intentions to kill his girlfriend were admissible under a dangerousness exception to the therapist privilege. *California v. Wharton*, 809 P.2d 290 (Cal. Sup. Ct. 1991), 15 MPDLR 397.

Impact of Disclosure

In *Doe v. New York Univ.*, 666 F.2d 761 (2d Cir. 1981), 6 MDLR 26, the Second Circuit overturned a preliminary injunction directing a medical school to readmit a student it had dismissed after her history of serious psychiatric problems became known. The university was allowed to use the student's mental impairment, substantiated by her psychiatric files, against her, since it was directly "relevant to her qualifications for readmission . . . and bears upon her ability to function as a student and doctor."

Privacy

Hawaii Psychiatric Soc. v. Ariyoshi, 481 F. Supp. 1028 (D. Hawaii 1979), 4 MDLR 19, found that Hawaii's administrative scheme allowing state auditors to search confidential psychiatric patient files was unconstitutional because it violated the patients' privacy rights. While acknowledging the state's legitimate interests in reviewing the records to prevent Medicaid fraud and abuse, the court held that the means employed were unnecessarily intrusive.

Liability

Psychiatrists, medical doctors, hospital staff, mental health facilities, and state or federal governments that provide mental health services can be held liable based on duties owed to patients/residents and to third parties. A practitioner may be liable to patients directly for decisions to detain, release, treat, or not treat, or to third parties when a current or former patient kills or injures someone. Often the individual treatment provider must be found liable before hospitals or government employers are deemed responsible. Questions of liability often are complicated by the issues of immunity, and standards of care owed to patients and third parties.

Residents/Patients

O'Connor v. Donaldson, 422 U.S. 563 (1975), 1 MDLR 336, held that a state hospital superintendent was personally liable for monetary damages for violating a patient's constitutional right to liberty. Liability was narrowly predicated on: (1) whether the superintendent "knew or reasonably should have known that the action he took within his sphere of official responsibility" would violate the patient's constitutional rights, or (2) whether "he took the action with the malicious intention to cause a deprivation of constitutional rights or injury" to the patient. This constitutional mandate has placed mental health professionals in a double bind: they risk liability if they do not release nondangerous individuals, and also if they release an individual who subsequently commits a violent act.

In the landmark decision of *Youngberg v. Romeo,* 457 U.S. 307 (1982), 6 MDLR 223, the U.S. Supreme Court established a restrictive institutional liability standard: courts must defer to the judgment of qualified professionals when considering an institution's liability. Moreover, "liability may be imposed only when the decision by the professional is such a substantial departure from accepted professional judgment, practice or standards as to demonstrate that the person responsible actually did not base the decision on such a judgment." *Id.* at 323.

Non-institution based malpractice suits generally allege a failure to provide proper treatment or to protect the patient from harm. In *DeShaney v. Winnebago County Dep't of Social Servs.*, 489 U.S. 189 (1989), 13 MPDLR 104, the U.S. Supreme Court found no duty to protect an abused child who was not in state custody. The duty to protect arises only when the state has limited a person's "freedom to act on his own behalf — through incarceration, institutionalization, or other similar restraint on personal liberty." *See also Philadelphia Police & Fire Ass'n for Handicapped Children, Inc. v. City of Philadelphia, supra* p. 49; *Monahan v. Dorchester Counseling Center, Inc.*, 770 F. Supp. 43 (D. Mass. 1991), 16 MPDLR 73; *Doe v. Douglas County School Dist. RE-1*, 770 F. Supp. 591 (D. Colo. 1991), 16 MPDLR 74; and *Fialkowski v. Greenwich Home for Children, Inc.*, 921 F.2d 459 (3d Cir. 1990), 15 MPDLR 283.

Suits alleging that mental health professionals have had sexual relations with their patients are on the rise. Common legal issues are whether the therapist was acting within the scope of his or her professional relationship, and whether the suit is timely. In *St. Paul Fire & Marine Ins. Co. v. Love*, 459 N.W.2d 698 (Minn. Sup. Ct. 1990), 15 MPDLR 80, the Minnesota supreme court held that an insurance carrier could be held liable if the sexual aspect of the therapist's conduct was "inextricably related to the professional services provided or withheld." Citing the situation in which a patient transfers feelings and behaviors onto the therapist, the court stated that "sexual conduct between therapist and patient arising from the [transference] phenomenon may be viewed as the consequence of a failure to provide proper treatment." *See also St. Paul Fire & Marine Ins. Co. v. D.H.L.*, 459 N.W.2d 704 (Minn. Sup. Ct. 1990), 15 MPDLR 80.

The Alabama supreme court ruled that the state was not liable to an involuntary patient who was sexually abused by her psychologist; the psychologist's acts were outside the scope of his state employment. *Doe v. Swift*, 570 So. 2d 1209 (Ala. Sup. Ct. 1990), 15 MPDLR 282.

Maryland's highest court held that a patient stated a cause of action for emotional distress against a psychologist who began a sexual relationship with the patient's wife. *Figueiredo-Torres v. Nickel*, 584 N.E.2d 69 (Md. Ct. App. 1991), 15 MPDLR 282.

Third Party Liability

Third party psychiatric liability actions generally arise when a discharged or escaped patient injures or kills another individual. While somewhat dated, the 1976 article "Getting Caught in the 'Open Door': Psychiatrists, Patients and Third Parties," 1 MDLR 220, provides a useful overview. "[T]he psychiatrist is not expected to make error-free diagnosis and release decisions; rather, what the courts expect are reasonable decisions based on a thorough review of the patient's case history." Furthermore, liability generally will not be imposed when psychiatrists can show that the patient's mental condition improved and that the release decision bore some reasonable relationship to the risk involved.

Liability generally requires findings that the doctor and/or facility had a duty to the third party, and that the harm was foreseeable. (*See* preceding discussion on duty to protect.) Foreseeability was the key issue in two state supreme court cases. In *Rollins v. Petersen*, 813 P.2d 1156 (Utah Sup. Ct. 1991), 15 MPDLR, no duty of care was found where a patient on unauthorized leave killed someone in a car accident. Similarly, in *Webb v. Jarvis*, 575 N.E.2d 992 (Ind. Sup. Ct. 1991), 15 MPDLR 600, it was unreasonable to expect a doctor to foresee either that the medication he prescribed would lead his patient to shoot his brother-in-law or that the victim was the patient's specific target.

A federal court ruled that the failure to control a VA patient by discharging him inappropriately can state a cause of action under the Federal Tort Claims Act, 28 U.S.C. §2680, when the patient harms a third party. *Mahomes-Vinson v. United States*, 751 F. Supp. 913 (D. Kan. 1990), 15 MPDLR 286. *See also Georgia Dep't of Human Resources v. Peeks*, 403 S.E.2d 36 (Ga. Sup. Ct. 1991), 15 MPDLR 399; *Ex parte Dale*, 581 So. 2d 479 (Ala. Sup. Ct. 1990), 15 MPDLR 287; *Thayer v. Jackson Brook Inst., Inc.*, 584 A.2d 653 (Me. Sup. Jud. Ct. 1991), 15 MPDLR 285; and *Amadon v. New York*, 565 N.Y.S.2d 677 (N.Y. Ct. Cl. 1990), 15 MPDLR 285.

Sovereign Immunity & Other Limits

Eleventh amendment sovereign immunity insulates states from federal court intervention. In *Pennhurst II*, 465 U.S. 89 (1984), 8 MPDLR 7, *supra* pp. 41, 47, the U.S. Supreme Court held that federal courts were prohibited from ordering state officials to conform their conduct to the requirements of state law. The Court later expanded this prohibition to cover any remedial actions, unless the state agreed to waive immunity by accepting the benefits of a federal law in which there is express language, an overwhelming textual implication, or an unequivocal expression that Congress intended such a consequence. *Atascadero State Hosp. v. Scanlon*, 473 U.S. 234 (1985), 9 MPDLR 270. *See also Lelsz v. Kavanagh*, 629 F. Supp. 1487 (N.D. Tex. 1986), *cert. denied*, 483 U.S. 1057 (1987), 10 MPDLR 175, *supra* p. 48, 50.

With or without a waiver of sovereign immunity, a federal court may grant prospective injunctive or declaratory relief against a state, even if compliance requires the expenditure of money, as long as monetary damages for past injuries are not awarded. *Brennan v. Stewart*, 834 F.2d 1248 (5th Cir. 1988), 12 MPDLR 185.

The eleventh amendment does not bar §1983 civil rights suits filed against state officials in their personal, as opposed to their official, capacities. Personal-capacity suits seek to impose individual liability for actions taken under color of state law, whereas official-capacity suits attempt to make the state liable for the official actions of a state employee/agent. *Hafer v. Melo*, 112 S. Ct. 358 (1991), 16 MPDLR 71.

Mental health professionals may also be protected by qualified immunity, which normally applies unless the defendant violated a patient's clearly established constitutional right, or was deliberately indifferent to a patient's medical needs. For example, there was no qualified immunity when an involuntary patient died after he was secluded in violation of his due process rights. *Hopper v. Callahan*, 562 N.E.2d 822 (Mass. Sup. Jud. Ct. 1990), 15 MPDLR 180. In contrast, qualified immunity applied in *Zwalesky v. Manistee*, 749 F. Supp. 815 (W.D. Mich. 1990), 15 MPDLR 182, because a prisoner had no clear constitutional right to be screened for psychological problems or suicidal tendencies. *See also Elliott v. Cheshire County, N.H.*, 750 F. Supp. 1146 (D.N.H. 1990), 15 MPDLR 181.

Professional Licensing & Discipline

A professional's mental disability may become an issue in a licensing or disciplinary action. Many of the reported cases involve attorneys and, as the authors noted in "Mentally Troubled Lawyers: Client Protection and Bar Discipline," 3 MDLR 179, the practitioner may argue that his mental condition renders him incompetent to defend against disciplinary charges, or he may defend himself by claiming that his condition made him unable to control his actions at the time of the alleged misconduct. *See also* "In Search of New Remedies: Mentally Disabled Doctors and the Practice of Medicine," 3 MDLR 428, concerning the approaches that the medical profession and various states have taken with respect to physicians impaired by mental illnesses.

When a practitioner raises a mental impairment as a defense, the disciplinary board and/or court generally focuses on whether the disability caused or contributed to the alleged misconduct and whether the person has or is willing to seek treatment. In such cases, a sanction less severe than disbarment or license revocation may be imposed, with readmission conditioned on successful treatment.

For example, West Virginia's supreme court found that some sort of mental disorder had likely caused an attorney's contemptuous and disruptive behavior, and held that he should be suspended for three months and undergo a psychiatric exam before being readmitted. *Committee on Legal Ethics of W. Va. State Bar v. Farber,* 408 S.E.2d 274 (W. Va. Sup. Ct. 1991), *cert. denied,* 112 S. Ct. 970 (1992), 16 MPDLR 77. Minnesota's highest court placed an attorney with severe depression on inactive status until he could show that he had overcome any disability that would prevent him from engaging in the competent and ethical practice of law. *In re Disciplinary Action Against Farrell,* 476 N.W.2d 165 (Minn. Sup. Ct. 1991), 16 MPDLR 209. And, Missouri's supreme court held that an attorney who had not sought treatment for a narcissistic psychological disorder could not be reinstated to practice law. *In re Jacobs,* 794 S.W.2d 199 (Mo. Sup. Ct. 1990), 15 MPDLR 84. *See also In re Disciplinary Proceedings Against Wolf,* 476 N.W.2d 878 (Wis. Sup. Ct. 1991), 16 MPDLR 209; *Cincinnati Bar Ass'n v. Weber,* 581 N.E.2d 519 (Ohio Sup. Ct. 1991), 16 MPDLR 209; *In re Reinstatement of Porter,* 472 N.W.2d 654 (Minn. Sup. Ct. 1991), 15 MPDLR 605; and *Attorney Grievance Comm'n of Maryland v. Bakas,* 593 A.2d 1087 (Md. Ct. App. 1991), 15 MPDLR 606.

Social Security Programs & Medicaid

Social Security

People with mental disabilities may be entitled to Social Security disability benefits (Title II) and to Supplemental Security Income (SSI) (Title XVI). Under both programs, the term "disability" refers to the "inability to engage in any substantial gainful activity by reason of any medically determinable physical or mental impairment which can be expected to result in death or which has lasted or can be expected to last for a continuous period of not less than twelve months." Applicants must also show that their impairment(s) is so severe that they not only cannot do their past work but, considering their age, education, and work experience, cannot engage in any other kind of substantial gainful work that exists in the national economy.

Mental Health Ass'n of Minn. v. Schweiker, 554 F. Supp. 157 (D. Minn. 1982), 7 MDLR 18, was the first in a series of nationwide decisions in which persons with severe mental illnesses successfully sought benefits under the SSI and Social Security disability insurance programs. The court issued a preliminary injunction requiring that eligibility determinations be made without employing "a presumption that an individual whose mental impairment is not as severe as those contained in the Listing of Impairments is capable of performing at least unskilled work." The Eighth Circuit affirmed this decision, in *Mental Health Ass'n of Minn. v. Heckler*, 720 F.2d 965 (8th Cir. 1983), 7 MDLR 455.

After many lawsuits were filed challenging benefit terminations and many people complained, Congress reviewed the Social Security disability system and enacted the 1984 Amendments. 42 U.S.C. §1305 et seq., 8 MPDLR 486. Under these provisions, benefit terminations require an actual improvement in the person's disabling condition, or substantial new evidence that the prior eligibility determination was erroneous. Moreover, an applicant with multiple impairments could not be denied benefits merely because none of those impairments alone was severe. Rather, consideration had to be given to the cumulative effects of those impairments. The 1984 amendments also declared a moratorium on reviews of mental impairments until new listings of mental conditions were prepared, and the Social Security Administration had to make every reasonable effort to use qualified psychiatrists or psychologists in evaluating claimants' mental impairments.

The Social Security Administration (SSA) promulgated new regulations to implement these amendments, establishing a five-step sequential process to evaluate an impairment's severity. Step one determines if the person is engaged in substantial gainful activity. Step two examines whether, without looking at age, education, and work experience, the person has a medically severe impairment or combination of impairments that limit his or her ability to do most work activities. If the person meets this threshold, then step three determines whether the impairment is equivalent to a number of listed impairments (the Medical-Vocational Guidelines, or "Grids") that are presumed to preclude substantial gainful activity. An applicant with an impairment that meets or is equivalent to a listed impairment is entitled to benefits. Otherwise, step four determines whether the person is able to perform his or her past relevant work. If not, then the final step evaluates whether, in light of the applicant's age, education, and work experience, he or she is able to perform other work that is available in the national economy. If not, the applicant is eligible for benefits.

In *Bowen v. Yuckert*, 482 U.S. 137 (1987), 11 MPDLR 277, the U.S. Supreme Court upheld this evaluation process, particularly the step-two severity determination, because it adopted a functional approach to determining the effects of medical impairments.

The Supreme Court struck down regulations that made children ineligible for benefits they would have received had they been adults. *Sullivan v. Zebley*, 493 U.S. 521 (1990), 14 MPDLR 175. The Social Security Act provided that children were eligible for benefits if they had an impairment of "comparable severity" to one that would entitle an adult to benefits. SSA's failure to allow a functional disability test for children, as it did for adults, created a more restrictive disability standard than the statute required. While a vocational assessment might be inappropriate for a child, an individualized functional analysis could be made which would consider the impairment's effects on the child's daily activities, such as speaking, walking, washing, dressing, eating, and playing.

In the wake of *Zebley*, the government issued two new disability regulations. First, SSA revised the listings to conform the definitions of major childhood mental disorders to those used by mental health professionals. The revised listing also created separate age-based categories, making it easier for SSA to evaluate infants and children between the ages of 1 and 3. Second, SSA must consider an impairment's cumulative effect on a child's daily life. Eligibility will be based not on the child's medical condition(s) alone, but also on his or her overall functioning, as measured by how well he or she can perform age-appropriate activities. *See* 55 Fed. Reg. 51208 (12/12/90), and 56 Fed. Reg. 5534 (2/11/91), 15 MPDLR 89.

The SSA also added Down syndrome to the listings used to determine if a child's impairment meets or equals the severity requirement. Children with Down syndrome previously were evaluated under the listing for mental retardation, which did not always produce accurate results, and often caused delays in evaluating infants from birth to six months, when it is difficult to evaluate the condition's manifestations. *See* 55 Fed. Reg. 51204 (12/12/90), 15 MPDLR 89.

Finally, SSA began sending notices to all children who were denied or who lost their benefits between January 1, 1980 and February 27, 1990, informing them of their right to have their claims re-evaluated under the new rules. The agency estimated that nearly 452,000 children may be entitled to reconsideration and could receive more than $2 billion in benefits. *See* 15 MPDLR 417.

In *Sullivan v. Finkelstein*, 496 U.S. 617 (1990), 14 MPDLR 435, the Supreme Court held that the Secretary of Health and Human Services could immediately appeal a federal district court's decision invalidating Social Security regulations and remanding a case for an eligibility determination without these regulations. As discussed earlier, the issue of when a Social Security decision is final is important with respect to the period within which a claimant has to apply for attorneys' fees under the Equal Access to Justice Act. *See* p. 15.

In *Johnson v. Sullivan*, 922 F.2d 346 (7th Cir. 1990), 15 MPDLR 293, the Seventh Circuit ended eight years of litigation by striking down the Secretary's policy of not considering the combined effects of non-severe impairments. The court held that the Supreme Court's decision upholding the severity regulation as a screening device, *Bowen v. Yuckert, supra,* did not address this issue.

The Seventh Circuit also held, in *Thompson v. Sullivan*, 933 F.2d 581 (7th Cir. 1991), 15 MPDLR 512, that a claimant who alleged multiple impairments, including alcoholism and depression, had not knowingly and intelligently waived his right to counsel at an eligibility hearing. Moreover, the administrative law judge should have taken additional steps to ensure the development of an adequate record, especially in light of the claimant's possible mental conditions. For a selection of recent rulings on Social Security disability benefits for persons with mental impairments, *see* 16 MPDLR 210-211, 15 MPDLR 294-95, 512, 607, and 14 MPDLR 177-80, 260-63, 436-37.

Representative Payee

A growing issue is the appointment of representative payees to receive and manage benefits on behalf of claimants who are deemed incapable of doing so on their own. While these appointments are designed to protect beneficiaries who might otherwise waste an important source of income or be vulnerable to abuse by others, the program has been attacked with respect to the standards and procedures used to determine incapability, the due process protections afforded beneficiaries, the screening and monitoring of persons appointed as representatives, and the suspension of benefits to persons for whom no qualified representative is found. *See Briggs v. Sullivan,* 886 F.2d 1132 (9th Cir. 1989), 14 MPDLR 64, and "Improving the Social Security Representative Payee Program — Recommendations of the Administrative Conference of the United States," 16 MPDLR 232.

Medicaid

Medicaid (Title XIX) is a joint federal-state medical assistance program for families with dependent children and aged, blind, or disabled individuals who meet a "means test," involving certain allowable levels of income and resources. As long as states follow the basic federal requirements, they have broad discretion to draw their programs to meet their residents' needs. States are reimbursed based on estimated future expenditures for covered services. While Medicaid litigation involving persons with mental disabilities is relatively infrequent, several cases deserve mention.

The U.S. Supreme Court held that the "overall character" of an intermediate care facility (ICF) made it an institution for mental diseases that is ineligible for Medicaid funding. *Connecticut Dep't of Income Maintenance v. Heckler,* 471 U.S. 524 (1985).

In *Homeward Bound v. The Hissom Memorial Center,* No. 85-C-437-E (N.D. Okla. July 24, 1987), 11 MPDLR 358, the Medicaid regulations governing intermediate care facilities for persons with mental retardation (ICF/MR) were used for the first time to create community services for institution residents. The federal court enforced requirements that residents be allowed to participate in daily community-based activities, that states develop discharge plans for all residents who did not need to be institutionalized, and that residents be given a wide-range of habilitative services to help them develop their life skills to the maximum extent possible. In *King v. Sullivan*, 776 F. Supp. 645 (D.R.I. 1991), 16 MPDLR 194, however, a court denied summary judgment to Medicaid recipients, finding that material issues of fact existed as to whether the state should be required to establish more community-based ICF/MR services.

The U.S. Supreme Court held that federal district courts have jurisdiction to review reimbursement denials made by the U.S. Department of Health and Human Services to state-owned ICF/MRs. *Bowen v. Massachusetts*, 487 U.S. 879 (1988), 12 MPDLR 536. Also, the 1980 Boren Amendment gives facilities the right to sue state officials under §1983 of the Civil Rights Act if Medicaid reimbursement rates are not "reasonable and adequate." *Wilder v. Virginia Hosp. Ass'n*, 496 U.S. 498 (1990), 14 MPDLR 432.

Miller v. Ibarra, 746 F. Supp. 19 (D. Colo. 1990), 15 MPDLR 169, held that income from judicially imposed trusts is not available to mentally incompetent nursing home patients for purposes of determining their Medicaid eligibility. *See also Klipfel v. Department of Social Servs.*, 804 S.W.2d 768 (Mo. Ct. App. 1990), 15 MPDLR 388.

Recently, litigation has involved reimbursement for Clozapine (trade name Clozaril), a relatively new drug prescribed for persons with chronic schizophrenia who have not responded to other treatment. Unlike other psychotropic medications, Clozapine does not cause tardive dyskinesia, an often debilitating, irreversible side-effect, but may cause a potentially fatal blood condition. Consequently, Sandoz Pharmaceuticals, the drug's manufacturer, required that patients who wish to take the drug participate in a prohibitively expensive blood-screening process (one year of drug and screening estimated to cost almost $9,000).

Still, several courts have held that state Medicaid programs must include Clozapine in their list of reimbursable drugs. For example, the court in *Visser v. Taylor*, 756 F. Supp. 501 (D. Kan. 1990), 14 MPDLR 528, issued a preliminary injunction prohibiting the state from denying Clozapine to a Medicaid recipient. The court found that the patient, whose schizophrenia manifested itself in suicidal delusions and hallucinations and had not responded to 10 different drugs, would suffer immediate irreparable harm without an injunction. Likewise, a New York trial court held that once the state Commissioner of Health acknowledged Clozapine's clinical value, he had no discretion to refuse to reimburse patients with schizophrenia for the drug, despite the potential impact on the state Medicaid budget. *Alexander L. v. Cuomo*, No. 40389/91 (N.Y. Sup. Ct. Apr. 4, 1991), 15 MPDLR 389. *See also Doe v. Palmer*, C90-4101 (N.D. Iowa Mar. 18, 1991), 16 MPDLR 194.

In July 1991, Sandoz entered into a consent decree with the Federal Trade Commission to settle charges that the company's marketing of Clozapine violated federal antitrust laws. Without admitting wrongdoing, Sandoz agreed to "unbundle" Clozapine from its costly blood monitoring program, so that doctors can no longer be forced to obtain monitoring through the program established by Sandoz. *See* 15 MPDLR 390. *See also* "New Directions in Mental Health Advocacy? Clozapine and the Right of Medical Self-Determination," 14 MPDLR 453.

PART III
Special Resources

ABA Commission on Mental & Physical Disability Law

The American Bar Association, through the Commission on Mental and Physical Disability Law, offers a wide assortment of resources to assist the lawyer/advocate who has a mental disability law practice. For more information on the Commission and the projects described below, including a catalog of products and services with a current price list, please call (202) 331-2240.

The ABA established the Commission on the Mentally Disabled in 1973 to help individuals with mental disabilities obtain adequate treatment in humane environments and to safeguard their basic legal rights. In 1991, the Commission was renamed the Commission on Mental and Physical Disability Law with an expanded mission to fulfill the ABA's commitment to justice and the rule of law for people with mental and physical disabilities. The Commission is a multidisciplinary group of lawyers, mental and physical disability professionals, administrators, and advocates. Over the years, the Commission has sponsored model advocacy projects in cooperation with local and state bar associations, developed a comprehensive series of model state developmental disability laws with detailed commentaries, and issued recommended practices in the civil commitment and guardianship areas.

Products & Services

Mental and Physical Disability Law Reporter

The Commission's longest-running project, the *Reporter* is a bimonthly journal and reporting service that has covered the legal, legislative, and regulatory developments in the rapidly expanding disability law field since 1976. While the *Reporter* is written to be understood by non-lawyers, the material is comprehensive and detailed in order to meet the legal practitioner's needs. Each issue analyzes 250 court decisions, including every important reported decision and many unpublished ones as well. An "Executive Summary and Analysis" summarizes the most important items contained in each issue, providing an overview of recent developments in the entire field, as well as quick access to particular areas of interest. Each issue also includes recent legislative and regulatory developments, and at least one special feature of interest to individuals working in the disability field — articles relating to "nuts and bolts" practice issues, the insanity defense, patients' rights, and model statutes, to name just a few.

Current and back issues of the *Reporter* provide a comprehensive overview of the field, and each court decision, and newly-enacted law or promulgated regulation is categorized according to a detailed subject matter index that provides a quick reference to specific areas of interest. A Ten-Year Index (1976-86) and cumulative annual supplements list cases alphabetically, as well as by subject matter and jurisdiction. In recent years, the *Reporter* added key word descriptors to supplement the key numbers.

Legal Research Services

The Commission provides legal research services on a fee-for-service basis. Information is gathered from a variety of sources, including the *Reporter* materials mentioned above, WESTLAW, LEXIS, LEGISLATE, PIE ON LINE, ABA/NET, the Library of Congress, and major universities, law schools and law firm libraries. Commission staff can conduct research for the public on a wide variety of disability topics. Case summaries, the full text of all the cases summarized in the *Reporter*, and reprints of articles can be ordered either singly, or as part of a computer search of all the materials on a particular topic.

Americans with Disabilities Act Manual

The Commission just published a manual that covers the Americans with Disabilities Act (ADA) in detail, including both the statute and the implementing regulations. The Manual provides general coverage of the entire act, as well as extensive coverage of

Titles I through III concerning employment, state and local government services, and public accommodations. The articles are intended for lawyers and nonlawyers alike, and provide legal analysis and numerous practical examples.

Court-Related Needs of the Elderly and Persons with Disabilities

Under a grant from the State Justice Institute, and in conjunction with the National Judicial College, the ABA convened the National Conference on Court-Related Needs of the Elderly and Persons with Disabilities in February 1991. This conference produced 75 recommendations aimed at creating a fully accessible judicial system. The recommendations were published with detailed commentary and other accompanying materials. The Commission, along with the ABA Commission on Legal Problems of the Elderly, continues to provide technical assistance to implement these recommendations.

The ADA and Persons with Mental Illnesses

The Commission and the National Mental Health Association recently received a grant from The Pew Charitable Trusts to educate employers about the ADA's employment provisions as they apply to people with mental illnesses. A related objective is to provide information about different types of mental illnesses, thereby dispelling common fears, stereotypes, and misconceptions that can lead to discrimination. The project will produce a resource manual for employers and provide technical assistance based on information gathered during the project. The grant is part of the Funding Partnership for People with Disabilities.

Task Force on Member Benefits for Lawyers with Disabilities

The ABA's Board of Governors appointed a task force to develop guidelines to increase access within the Association for lawyers with disabilities. At the ABA's August 1992 Annual Meeting, the Task Force will present guidelines and recommendations on specific steps the Association can take to make the ABA's membership, programs and services more accessible to lawyers with disabilities.

HIV/AIDS

In conjunction with the ABA Center for Children and the Law, the Commission examined the AIDS-related legal issues affecting persons with developmental disabilities. With funding from the U.S. Department of Health and Human Services, the project published *AIDS and Persons with Developmental Disabilities: The Legal Perspective* (1990), focusing on a broad range of issues, particularly discrimination, testing, quarantine, civil commitment, and federal entitlement programs. The Commission also published *AIDS/HIV and Confidentiality: Model Policy and Procedures* (1991), the first comprehensive model confidentiality policy for programs and agencies serving individuals with HIV infection.

Involuntary Civil Commitment — A Manual for Lawyers and Judges

A comprehensive manual that introduces an approach that encourages lawyers and judges to become involved before the commitment hearing, using pre-hearing screening, negotiation, and diversion into less restrictive alternatives to reduce the number of full court hearings. The manual provides a concise overview of civil commitment practices; gives a step-by-step guide for attorneys with clients facing commitment; addresses the commitment process from the perspective of the attorney representing the interests of the state or the petitioner; and comprehensively examines the judge's role and responsibilities. Also includes a general involuntary commitment interview and strategy form, and charts of selected statutory provisions nationwide.

Steps to Enhance Guardianship Monitoring

With funding from the State Justice Institute, the Commission and the Commission on Legal Problems of the Elderly published a comprehensive set of recommendations to improve court supervision of guardians and conservators. This 1991 report sets out 10 steps in the monitoring process, including requiring that guardians file reports on their ward's financial and personal status; developing training materials to help guardians carry out their duties; and investigating problems that arise during a guardianship.

Charts tabulating every jurisdiction's guardianship provisions, from initiation through termination, are included.

Guardianship —An Agenda For Reform

Based on the ABA's 1988 National Guardianship Symposium, this monograph presents 33 recommendations with commentary on ways to improve the nation's guardianship system in the areas of due process, determining incapacity, judicial practices, accountability of guardians, and the role of guardianship agencies. Thirty one of the recommendations, set out separately in an appendix, were adopted by the ABA's House of Delegates as official ABA policy.

Life Services Planning

With funding from the U.S. Department of Health and Human Services, and in conjunction with the ABA's Commission on Legal Problems of the Elderly, the Commission issued several publications concerning long-range planning for elderly people and people with disabilities and their families. Topics include estate and financial planning, and planning for incapacity, including advance health care directives, and other guardianship alternatives.

TABLE OF CASES

Abney ex rel. Kantor v. District of Columbia ... 78
Adams v. Alderson ... 74
Addington v. Texas ... 22
Adult Group Properties, Ltd. v. Imler ... 65
Ake v. Oklahoma ... 39
Alexander v. Choate ... 73
Alexander L. v. Cuomo ... 100
Allen v. Heckler ... 76
Amadon v. New York ... 92
Andersen v. District of Columbia ... 80
ARC of North Dakota v. Olson ... 43
Arkansas v. Sypult ... 88
Ash v. Lake Oswego School Dist. No. 7J ... 80
Atascadero State Hosp. v. Scanlon ... 51, 82, 92
Attorney Grievance Comm'n of Maryland v. Bakas ... 94
Barefoot v. Estelle ... 32
Barlow-Gresham Union High School Dist. No. 2 v. Mitchell ... 14
Barton-Malow Co., Inc. v. Wilburn ... 58
Bee v. Greaves ... 46
Billotti v. Dodrill ... 36
Blake v. Kemp ... 39
Blue Shield of Va. v. McCready ... 85
Blum v. Stenson ... 13
Board of Educ. of the Hendrick Hudson Central School Dist. v. Rowley ... 77
Board of Educ., Sacramento City Unified School Dist. v. Holland ... 79
Boggs, In re ... 23
Boggs v. New York City Health & Hosps. Corp. ... 23
Bowen v. Galbreath ... 15
Bowen v. Massachusetts ... 99
Bowen v. Yuckert ... 96
Bradley Center v. Wessner ... 86
Brady v. Hopper ... 87
Brennan v. Stewart ... 93
Brewer v. Lincoln Nat'l Life Ins. Co. ... 84
Briggs v. Sullivan ... 98
Brooks v. Johnson & Johnson, Inc. ... 41
Buckner v. United States ... 43
Burchell v. Dep't of the Army ... 75
Burka v. New York City Transit Auth. ... 74
Burr ex rel. Burr v. Ambach ... 80
Bussey v. Kentucky ... 33
Butler v. Thornburgh ... 75
California v. Wharton ... 89
Canales v. Sullivan ... 58
Carey ex rel. Carey v. Maine School Admin. Dist. 17 ... 81
Carter v. Tisch ... 75
Caswell v. Secretary of Health & Human Servs. ... 44
Chasse v. Mazerolle ... 55
Chester Upland School Dist. v. Lester H. ... 80
Chichackly v. United States ... 31
Chris C. v. Gwinnett County School Dist. ... 79
Christenson v. Georgia ... 39
Christopher M. v. Corpus Christi Indep. School Dist. ... 81

Christopher W. v. Portsmouth School Comm. 81
Cincinnati Bar Ass'n v. Weber 94
City of Cleburne v. Cleburne Living Center, Inc. 65
City of Livonia v. Dep't of Social Servs. 65
Civitans Care, Inc. v. Board of Adjustment of the City of Huntsville 65
Clark v. Cohen 50
Cleveland v. Central Bank of the South 57
Clovis Unified School Dist. v. California Office of Admin. Hearings 80
Cole v. Taylor 87
Colorado v. Branch 28
Colorado v. Connelly 30
Colorado v. Medina 45
Colorado v. Serravo 34
Colorado ex rel. M.K.M. 60
Commitment of S.L., In re 24
Committee on Legal Ethics of W. Va. State Bar v. Farber 94
Connecticut Dep't of Income Maintenance v. Heckler 98
Consolidated Rail Corp. v. Darrone 71
Copeland v. Philadelphia Police Dep't 74
Cordrey v. Euckert 80
Cowley v. Stricklin 39
Cruzan v. Director, Missouri Dep't of Health 61
Cuevas v. Collins 31
Currie v. United States 87
Custody of a Minor 63
Dale, Ex parte 92
Daley v. Koch 73
Dellmuth v. Muth 82
D.E.R. v. La Crosse County 51
Derrick v. Peterson 31
DeShaney v. Winnebago County Dep't of Social Servs. 49, 90
Detention of Schuoler, In re 60
Developmental Disabilities Advocacy Center, Inc. v. Melton 10
Disciplinary Action Against Farrell, In re 94
Disciplinary Proceedings Against Wolf, In re 94
Dixon ARC v. Thompson 43
Doe v. Alabama Dep't of Educ. 80
Doe v. Douglas County School Dist. RE-1 90
Doe v. New York Univ. 89
Doe v. Palmer 100
Doe v. Public Health Trust of Dade County 26, 48
Doe v. Swift 91
Donaldson v. O'Connor 42
Donaldson v. Van de Camp 62
Double D Manor, Inc. v. Evergreen Meadows Homeowners' Ass'n 65
Dow v. Sullivan 16
D.R., In re 57
D.R. v. Daughters of Miriam Center for the Aged 56
Drew v. Clarke County School Dist. 80
Duane M. v. Orleans Parish School Bd. 14
Durham v. United States 34
Dusky v. United States 29
Eggers v. Bullitt 14
Eichner, In re 61
Elliott v. Cheshire County, N.H. 93

107

Estate of Hendrickson, In re	58
Estate of Loomis, In re	58
Estate of Raney, In re	57
Estelle v. Smith	28, 32
Evans v. Jeff D.	13
Familystyle of St. Paul, Inc. v. City of St. Paul	67
Farrell, In re	62
Fasulo v. Arafeh	23
Ferguson v. United States Dep't of Commerce	75
Fialkowski v. Greenwich Home for Children, Inc.	90
Fields v. Lyng	74
Figueiredo-Torres v. Nickel	91
Fleming v. Zant	32
Ford v. Gaither	40
Ford v. Wainwright	31
Foucha v. Louisiana	36
Franklin v. Gwinnett County Public Schools	82
Franklin v. U.S. Postal Serv.	74
Fuller v. Frank	75
Garrity v. Gallen	51
Gault, In re	18
G.D. v. Westmoreland School Dist.	80
Georgia Dep't of Human Resources v. Peeks	92
Germantown Ins. Co. v. Martin	85
Gilliland v. Carpenter	58
Greer v. Rome City School Dist.	79
Grinker, In re	53
Guardianship of Browning, In re	62
Guardianship of K.M., In re	56
Guardianship of Weedon	62
Guice-Mills v. Derwinski	75
Gutierrez v. Sullivan	16
Hafer v. Melo	93
Halderman v. Pennhurst State School & Hosp.	47
Hamel v. Brooks	24
Harris v. Indiana	37
Harris v. Vasquez	40
Hawaii Psychiatric Soc. v. Ariyoshi	89
Hayes, In re	55
Hayes v. Unified School Dist. No. 377	81
Hedlund v. Superior Court of Orange County	87
Henderson v. Dugger	40
Hensley v. Eckerhart	13
Homeward Bound v. The Hissom Memorial Center	49, 98
Honig v. Doe	81
Hopper v. Callahan	93
Hudson v. Sullivan	16
Idaho v. Rhoades	35
Idaho v. Searcy	35
Idaho v. Soura	33
Illinois v. Bernasco	31
Illinois v. Christy	30
Illinois v. Finkle	38
Illinois v. Pembrock	38
Irving Indep. School Dist. v. Tatro	78

Jablonski v. United States 86
Jackson v. Fort Stanton Hosp. & Training School 43
Jackson v. Indiana 29
Jacobs, In re 94
Jane Doe, In re 56
Jarvis v. Levine 45
Jefferson County Bd. of Educ. v. Breen 79
Jobes, In re 63
Johnson v. Bismarck Public School Dist. 14
Johnson v. Independent School Dist. No. 4 of Bixby, Tulsa County, Okla. 80
Johnson v. Sullivan 97
Jones v. United States 36
Jorgensen v. Indiana 88
J.S., In re 27, 57
Kansas v. Baker 36
Kansas v. Hill 38
Kansas v. William 31
K.B. v. Sprenger 24
Kentucky ARC v. Conn 51
Keyhea v. Rushen 46
King v. Sullivan 99
Klipfel v. Department of Social Servs. 99
Kordenbrock v. Scroggy 40
Kunin v. Benefit Trust Life Ins. Co. 84
Lassiter v. Dep't of Social Servs. of Durham County 10
Leland v. Oregon 35
Lelsz v. Kavanagh 48, 50, 92
Lesley, In re 27
Lessard v. Schmidt 22
Lester H. v. Gilhool 80
Liles v. Saffle 40
Lillian F. v. Superior Court of Cal. 60
Lipari v. Sears Roebuck & Co. 86
Little v. Armontrout 40
Long v. Iowa 31
Lovelace v. Keohane 58
Lynch v. Baxley 23
Mahomes-Vinson v. United States 92
Marbrunak, Inc. v. City of Stow, Ohio 67
Martin v. Ohio 35
Martin v. Wainwright 40
Maull v. Community Living for the Handicapped, Inc. 65
Max M. v. Thompson 78
May v. Sullivan 16
McKay v. Bergstedt 62
McKinney v. McKinney 56
Medina v. California 29
Melkonyan v. Sullivan 15
Mental Health Ass'n of Minn. v. Heckler 95
Mental Health Ass'n of Minn. v. Schweiker 95
Metropolitan Life Ins. Co. v. Massachusetts 83
Michigan v. Miller 30
Miller v. District Court 88
Miller v. Ibarra 99
Mills v. Rogers 45

Milteer, Ex parte 36
Minnesota ex rel. Pearson v. Probate Court 17
Miranda v. Arizona 30
Mississippi Protection & Advocacy Sys. v. Cotten 10
Moe, In re 56
Monahan v. Dorchester Counseling Center, Inc. 90
Mongony v. Bevilacqua 65
Montana v. Korell 35
Moore v. Brown 58
Moore v. District of Columbia 14
Moore v. Kemp 39
Moser v. DeSetta 58
Mrs. C. v. Wheaton 80
Nationwide Mutual Fire Ins. Co. v. May 85
Nebraska v. B.P. 56
Nebraska v. Harris 39
Nelson v. Thornburgh 72
New Hampshire v. Sarette 31
New Jersey v. Breakiron 38
New Jersey v. Moore 38
New Jersey v. Ogelsby 38
New Jersey v. Olivio 33
New Jersey v. Worlock 34
New Mexico v. Neely 37
New York ARC v. Carey 43
North Carolina v. Lloyd 39
North Carolina v. Sanchez 31
North Carolina Dep't of Transp. v. Crest St. Community Council, Inc. 14
O'Connor, In re 61
O'Connor v. Donaldson 22, 42, 47, 90
Ogle, Ex parte 57
Ohio v. Powell 39
O'Neal v. Division of Family Servs. 58
Oregon Psychological Ass'n v. Physicians Ass'n of Clackamas County, Inc. 85
Ortiz v. Texas 33
Pandazides v. Virginia Bd. of Educ. 74
Pape v. Byrd 58
Parham v. J.R. 10, 26
Pate v. Robinson 28
Pennhurst State School & Hosp. v. Halderman 41, 47, 92
Penry v. Lynaugh 32
Permian Basin Centers for Mental Health & Mental Retardation v. Alsobrook 65
Pesterfield v. Tennessee Valley Auth. 74
Peter, In re 63
Petersen v. Mutual Life Ins. Co. of N.Y. 84
Philadelphia Police & Fire Ass'n for Handicapped Children, Inc. v. City of Philadelphia 49, 90
Phillips v. Lincoln Nat'l Life Ins. Co. 84
Polk v. Central Susquehanna Intermediate Unit 16 78
Price v. Brittain 41
Price v. Sheppard 59
Project Release v. Prevost 46
R.A.D., In re 57
Rasmussen v. Fleming 63
Rector v. Clark 31
Reinking v. Philadelphia Am. Life Ins. Co. 84

Reinstatement of Porter, In re 94
Rennie v. Klein 46
Residential Management Systems, Inc. v. Jefferson County Plan Comm'n 65
Rhode Island v. Lopez 33
Rhode Island Dep't of Mental Health, Retardation & Hosps. v. R.B. 24
Rhodes v. Palmetto Pathway Homes, Inc. 64
Riese v. St. Mary's Hosp. & Medical Center 45
Riggins v. Nevada 29
Rivers v. Katz 46
R.J.D. v. Vaughan Clinic, P.C. 27
Robbins v. Budke 10
Rodgers v. Lehman 75
Rogers v. Commissioner of the Dep't of Mental Health 45
Rogers v. Frito Lay, Inc. 72
Rogers v. Okin 45
Rollins v. Petersen 92
Romero, In re 55
Rosa M., In re 60
Saffle v. Liles 40
Santosky v. Kramer 57
Satterwhite v. Texas 32
School Bd. of Nassau County, Fla. v. Arline 69, 73
School Comm. of the Town of Burlington v. Department of Educ. of Mass. 79, 81
Schuster v. Attenberg 87
Scott v. Plante 43
S.H. v. Edwards 43
Shaw v. Glickman 87
Shea v. Tisch 75
Shelter Mut. Ins. Co. v. Williams 84
Shirey v. Devine 75
Shoals Ford, Inc. v. Clardy 58
Smith v. McCormick 39
Smith v. Robinson 14
Smith v. United States 34
Society for Goodwill to Retarded Children, Inc. v. Cuomo 43, 49
South Carolina v. Wilson 37
Southeastern Community College v. Davis 70, 72
Specht v. Patterson 38
St. Paul Fire & Marine Ins. Co. v. D.H.L. 91
St. Paul Fire & Marine Ins. Co. v. Love 91
State Farm Fire & Casualty Co. v. Wicka 85
Storar, In re 62
Strathie v. Dep't of Transp. 72
Subpoena Served Upon Zuniga, In re 88
Sullivan v. Finkelstein 97
Sullivan v. Hudson 15
Sullivan v. Sullivan 16
Sullivan v. Zebley 96
Superintendent of Belchertown State School v. Saikewicz 62
Tarasoff v. Board of Regents of the Univ. of Cal. 86
Tarpley, In re 25
Thayer v. Jackson Brook Inst., Inc. 92
Thomas S. v. Flaherty 43
Thomas S. v. Morrow 50
Thompson v. Sullivan 97

111

Tiller v. Esposito ... 31
Timothy W. v. Rochester, N.H. School Dist. ... 78
Todd D. v. Andrews ... 78
Traynor v. Turnage ... 73
Trinidad v. Secretary of Health & Human Servs. ... 16
United States v. Bodey ... 28
United States v. Bradshaw ... 30
United States v. Charters ... 29, 44
United States v. Devin ... 33
United States v. Fonner ... 32
United States v. Gentry ... 32
United States v. Haga ... 31
United States v. LaFromboise ... 37
United States v. Moore ... 33
United States v. Nichelson ... 28
United States v. Poff ... 32
United States v. Pryce ... 33
United States v. Puerto Rico ... 67
United States v. Ruklick ... 32
United States v. Southern Management Corp. ... 66
United States v. Twine ... 38
United States ex. rel. Butler v. Bara ... 31
United States ex. rel. Stachulak v. Coughlin ... 39
Utah v. Anderson ... 37
Utah v. Hodges ... 39
Utley, In re ... 25
Valerie J. v. Derry Co-op School Dist. ... 80
Vermont v. Curtis ... 88
Vermont v. Mace ... 39
Village of Euclid v. Ambler Realty Co. ... 64
Village of Maywood v. Health, Inc. ... 65
Visser v. Taylor ... 100
Vitek v. Jones ... 10, 28
Wall v. Indiana ... 37
Washington v. Harper ... 29, 44
Webb v. Jarvis ... 92
Weber v. Stony Brook Hosp. ... 63
West Virginia v. Merritt ... 33
West Virginia Dep't of Human Servs. v. Peggy F. ... 56
West Virginia Univ. Hosps. v. Casey ... 14
Whitlock v. Donovan ... 75
Wilder v. Virginia Hosp. Ass'n ... 99
Williams v. Bowen ... 15
Williams v. Wilzack ... 46
Wisconsin Coalition for Advocacy, Inc. v. Gudeman ... 10
Wisconsin ex rel. Jones v. Gerhardstein ... 46
Woe v. Cuomo ... 43
Wyatt v. Aderholt ... 41
Wyatt v. King ... 23
Wyatt v. Stickney ... 41, 44
Yiadom v. Kiley ... 30
Youngberg v. Romeo ... 42, 90
Zinermon v. Burch ... 22, 26, 42
Zwalesky v. Manistee ... 93